DAWN OF A NEW DAY
THE NEW YORK WORLD'S FAIR
1939/40

DAWN OF A NEW DAY
THE NEW YORK WORLD'S FAIR, 1939/40

HELEN A. HARRISON,
Guest Curator

Essays by:

Joseph P. Cusker
Helen A. Harrison
Francis V. O'Connor
Eugene A. Santomasso
Warren I. Susman

THE QUEENS MUSEUM
NEW YORK UNIVERSITY PRESS · NEW YORK · LONDON

This exhibition is made possible by a major grant from
the National Endowment for the Humanities, a federal agency.
It is also made possible by grants from the New York Council for the Humanities
and the New York State Council on the Arts.

Cover Photograph: Harold Zipkowitz
Lightbulb with Trylon and Perisphere filament.
Lent by Arthur Cohen

DAWN OF A NEW DAY
THE NEW YORK
WORLD'S FAIR 1939/40

June 21-November 30, 1980

Library of Congress Catalogue Card No. 80-51839

ISBN 0-9604514-0-4 (HC, Queens Museum)
0-9604514-1-2 (PB, Queens Museum)

ISBN 8147-3407-3 (HC, N.Y.U. Press)
8147-3408-1 (PB, N.Y.U. Press)

Copyright © 1980 by
THE QUEENS MUSEUM
New York City Building
Flushing Meadow-Corona Park
Flushing, New York 11368

Catalogue Editor: Sara Blackburn
Art Director: Richard Haymes
Designer: Menny Borovski
Composition: Professional Typographic
    Services Inc.
Printer: Canterbury Press

Audio/Visual Presentation: Arcane Visuals, Ltd.

Printed in the United States of America.

Co-published by The Queens Museum, New York and
New York University Press, New York/London.

Half Title page:
Mayor La Guardia and Harvey Gibson welcome Fair visitors. (NYP)

Opposite Title page:
The Fairgrounds seen from midtown Manhattan. (NYP)

President Roosevelt visits the Fairgrounds
to lay the cornerstone of the U.S. Government Building,
June 30, 1938. (FC)

First trees arrive for planting
at the New York World's Fair. (FC)

In all of recorded history there are few periods as momentous as those watershed years, 1939-1940. While America was emerging slowly from the Great Depression, here at Flushing Meadow-Corona Park—and all across the country—dreams were spun about building the World of Tomorrow

Characteristic of the naiveté of that time was America's confidence in herself and her ability to forge a better tomorrow. This idea remained unquestioned even while tomorrow was dawning under dark and threatening clouds across the Atlantic.

Helene Margaret expressed the spirit of the time admirably in the final stanza of her prize-winning poem, "Tomorrow, America":*

> Here in these halls of science,
>   Here in these towers of art
> We have built the true defiance
>   And girded the nation's heart,
> Not with enduring stone
>   Or muscles that twist with pain,
> But with fires that burn
>   A vision in the brain.
> The tri-colored flag was cut
>   For us with subtle shears.
> No doors we open can shut
>   In a hundred thousand years.

In the forty years since, the world has learned much. Even the most futuristic predictions of technological progress made by exhibitors at the 1939/1940 World's Fair are tame compared to the reality of our strides forward—from plastic money to the conquest of outer space to the miracle of the CAT scan—and much, much more. And, while social change indeed was in the wind during those unforgettable years, that change was to be far more profound than anyone could have imagined.

The price of fundamentally restructuring the world as we knew it then has been awesome. The lives of millions of men, women, and children the world over had been directly touched. Nonetheless, I doubt that anyone would want to turn back the clock.

In the forty years since the Fair, many of the promises held out to us then have been fulfilled. We have seen the eradication of polio and smallpox, the end of legally sanctioned discrimination because of race, religion, sex, or national origin, a degree of prosperity beyond the wildest imagination of the most idealistic reformers of yesteryear.

Those forty years have taught us that man's scientific and technological progress does not—cannot—replace the primacy of sound human relationships among individuals and among nations as the basis for a satisfying existence.

Once we believed America to be omnipotent and omniscient; we now know differently. But we also know that those qualities are not the ones which make greatness. Rather, it is the fostering of individual freedom and individual opportunity that makes nations and their inhabitants thrive.

On these counts, the promise of America has been delivered beyond our fondest hopes. This Museum, whose staff and board members represent such diverse origins, is a small example, but one for which we must all be grateful.

On behalf of the Board of Trustees of The Queens Museum, I would like to express heartfelt thanks to the National Endowment for the Humanities for their extraordinary faith in this institution and in our World's Fair project. They have made it possible for us to take a giant step forward.

Our esteem and gratitude is expressed to Robert Moses, Honorary Chairman of the exhibition. The conversion of Flushing Meadow-Corona Park from F. Scott Fitzgerald's "valley of ashes" to a great urban recreational center, the site of two world's fairs, is only one of many significant public works of his extraordinary career.

Our thanks go to the Department of Cultural Affairs of the City of New York and the New York State Council on the Arts for their ongoing support of the Museum's programs.

Important as funding is, it cannot take the place of the imagination, dedication, and perseverance it took to mount this World's Fair exhibition and its accompanying events. For that—and so much more—the entire board gives its thanks, its admiration, and its love to Janet Schneider, Executive Director of The Queens Museum, who has brought together and inspired some of the best young talent of this age to help us better understand a bygone era.

Peter L. Rothholz
Chairman of the Board of Trustees
April 21, 1980

* Helene Margaret was one of five poets whose work was published by The Academy of American Poets in *The Official Poem of the 1939 New York World's Fair* and *Other Prize-Winning Poems.* (Bowne & Co., 44 pp.)

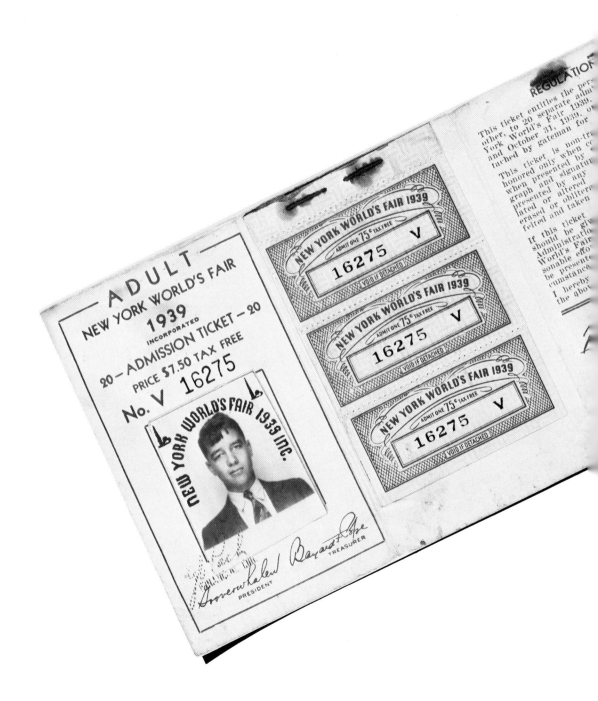

ADULT
NEW YORK WORLD'S FAIR
1939
INCORPORATED
20 — ADMISSION TICKET — 20
PRICE $7.50 TAX FREE
No. V 16275

NEW YORK WORLD'S FAIR 1939 INC.

Grover Whalen
PRESIDENT

Bayard Pope
TREASURER

NEW YORK WORLD'S FAIR 1939
ADMIT ONE 75¢ TAX FREE
V
16275
VOID IF DETACHED

NEW YORK WORLD'S FAIR 1939
ADMIT ONE 75¢ TAX FREE
V
16275
VOID IF DETACHED

NEW YORK WORLD'S FAIR 1939
ADMIT ONE 75¢ TAX FREE
V
16275
VOID IF DETACHED

REGULATIONS

This ticket entitles the person...
other, to 20 separate admis...
York World's Fair, 1939,...
and October 31, 1939, o...
tached by gateman for...

This ticket is non-tr...
honored only when co...
when presented by...
graph and signatur...
presented by any...
lated or altered...
erased or oblitera...
feited and taken...

If this ticket...
should be giv...
Administratio...
World's Fair...
sonable effor...
be present...
cumstance...
I hereby...
the abov...

CONTENTS

FOREWORD	Peter L. Rothholz	VI
ACKNOWLEDGEMENTS	Janet Schneider Helen A. Harrison	X
INTRODUCTION	Helen A. Harrison	I
THE WORLD OF TOMORROW: Science, Culture, and Community at the New York World's Fair	Joseph P. Cusker	3
THE PEOPLE'S FAIR: Cultural Contradictions of a Consumer Society	Warren I. Susman	17
THE DESIGN OF REASON: Architecture and Planning at the 1939/40 New York World's Fair	Eugene A. Santomasso	29
THE FAIR PERCEIVED: Color and Light as Elements in Design and Planning	Helen A. Harrison	43
THE USABLE FUTURE: The Role of Fantasy in the Promotion of a Consumer Society for Art	Francis V. O'Connor	57
CATALOGUE OF THE EXHIBITION	Helen A. Harrison	73

ACKNOWLEDGMENTS

Forty years ago a great drama was playing to its close on the fields of Flushing Meadow. However, the memory of the 1939/1940 New York World's Fair and the message of the Fair planners remains indelibly imprinted on the American consciousness. Only two buildings erected for that ambitious enterprise survive: the Aquacade, which attracted one of every six visitors to the Fair, and the New York City Building, which now houses The Queens Museum.

Dawn of a New Day: The New York World's Fair 1939/40 is more than a commemoration of that notable event. On a scholarly level, the exhibition represents a first attempt to analyze and interpret the Fair as a "cultural document" and a shaping influence on modern America. On a symbolic level, the exhibition heralds the opening of the Museum's newly renovated and expanded facilities. The second floor halls of the New York City Building, dark and unused for over fifteen years, reopen to the light of day and the light of art with this exhibition.

The Queens Museum is grateful to the individuals, organizations, and institutions that have helped transform the World's Fair project from idea to public event. To all those who have expressed their support—in the form of letters and telephone calls—who cannot be mentioned here, we extend our warmest thanks.

The project began in February 1979 through an initial research grant from the New York State Council on the Arts. The planning phase gathered momentum in July when additional support was obtained in the form of a grant from the National Endowment for the Humanities. We remember with gratitude the advice and enthusiasm of Andrea Anderson of the National Endowment for the Humanities, Joan Rosenbaum of the New York State Council on the Arts, Nora Mandel of Queens Borough Hall,

and Martin Beller of the New York Council for the Humanities, all of whom encouraged us to develop the project further.

Major funding from the National Endowment for the Humanities in April 1980 allowed the implementation of the exhibition and the publication of this catalogue. To the Chairman of the Endowment, Joseph D. Duffey, as well as its staff and advisors, we express our sincere appreciation. Public programming for the exhibition in the form of films, lectures, a symposium, and other special events, has been supported by the New York Council for the Humanities under the direction of Dr. Carol Groneman.

The Queens Museum was most fortunate to locate as Project Director a woman of extraordinary ability, Helen A. Harrison. Her talent, patience, and sheer tenacity in the face of an enormous task of research and organization continue to inspire those who have had the pleasure of working with her. Advising Ms. Harrison during both planning and implementation phases of the project has been a committee of three scholars: chief advisor, Warren I. Susman, and project advisors Francis V. O'Connor and Eugene A. Santomasso. Their valuable participation, as well as that of Joseph Cusker, has enriched both the exhibition and its catalogue.

The Museum is equally fortunate to have as a member of its staff Shelley Jane Grossberg, Assistant Director for Development. She has played a major role shaping the structure of the project and has integrated the work of the project staff, consultants, and museum personnel. In addition, her supervision of the various grant applications and her expertise in the preparation of accompanying financial documents have been essential to the success of the project. Other members of The Queens Museum staff whose efforts merit special mention are: Susan Lubowsky, who coordinated graphics, catalogue production, and distribution; Janet Katz, who supervised public programs; Deborah Silverfine, who researched and developed the exhibition film program.

The skill and imagination of several consultants has done much to enhance the exhibition. For their outstanding work, as well as for their patience under pressure, we thank Murry Gelberg, exhibition designer; Sara Blackburn, catalogue editor; Richard Haymes, catalogue designer; Dan Eisnitz of Arcane Visuals, developers of the exhibition slide show.

The success of the exhibition was linked directly to the completion of the Museum's renovation. Constant vigilance in the supervision of the construction process was of key importance. For this we say a special word of thanks to Bob Plushnick and Chris Piraino of the Department of General Services of the City of New York and James Frederico of Jenkins Contracting Company, for getting the job done.

Finally, I would like to express my admiration for the Board of Trustees of The Queens Museum, our policy-makers, and to the Honorable Donald R. Manes, President of the Borough of Queens, for the vision to see in the first steps of The Queens Museum the promise of a major cultural institution.

Janet Schneider
Executive Director
April 21, 1980

o thank the great number of people who have contributed to the making of this exhibition would be a happy but impossible task. It has been my pleasure to speak with many individuals who remember the Fair (as I do not) and whose reminiscences, anecdotes, insights, and advice have helped to shape both the form and content of the exhibition. To them, and to others who wrote and called to offer information and material for inclusion, I wish to express my sincere gratitude.

The members of the Advisory Committee—Warren I. Susman, Eugene A. Santomasso, and Francis V. O'Connor—whose outstanding backgrounds in humanistic scholarship enabled them to identify and develop the exhibition's themes have been a continuing inspiration. Without their guidance, the tasks of interpreting the vast amount of source material relating to the Fair and of locating and selecting the objects for exhibition would have been overwhelming

Our first source of research material was the late Frank Pokorney, historian, collector, friend to the Museum for many years, and one who is sorely missed by those of us who had the pleasure of working with him in the initial stages of research. Special thanks are also owing to Peter Warner, who generously made available his extensive collection of Fair documentation for both research and exhibition purposes; and to Frank Cronican, master model builder, collector, and World's Fair enthusiast, who kindly gave much time and interest to the project. The early advice and encouragement of Larry Zim, whose collection relating to many fairs was put at my disposal, is also very much appreciated.

Conversations with Donald Deskey, Frederick Gutheim, Wallace K. Harrison, Ray Lester, Dorothy Miller, Lewis Mumford, and Ian Woodner helped to clarify some points and raise others in the various phases of research. Interviews with artists Lucienne Bloch, Ilya Bolotowsky, Seymour Fogel, Balcomb Greene, Harold Lehman, Michael Loew, Thomas Lo Medico, Anton Refregier, Louis Schanker, and Stuyvesant Van Veen yielded insights into the Fair's decorative projects and resulted in the location of much original material, some of it never before exhibited.

In addition to the lenders and donors, who are listed in a separate section, others who have contributed to research and the location of material include: David Baxley, Triborough Bridge and Tunnel Authority; Lance Bird and Tom Johnson, An American Portrait; Lorraine Brown, Federal Theatre Archive; Davis Ehrhardt, Long Island Collection, Queens Borough Public Library; Joan Capelin and Richard Straub, Haines, Lundberg and Waehler; Lisa Cermak, Portledge School; Joseph Cottichio, Department of Parks; Crosley Collectors Club; Rachel Elkind, Tempi Productions; Susan Fogel, Parsons Brinkerhoff; George Gardner, Museum of Natural History; John F.H. Gorton, Rockwell Kent Legacies; Bernard Haber, Hardesty and Hanover; Robert Kaufmann, Cooper-Hewitt Museum, Smithsonian Institution; Sandra Kitt, Hayden Planetarium; Garnett McCoy and William McNaught,

Archives of American Art; Stephen Miller, Museum of the City of New York; Roger Mohovach, New-York Historical Society; Edward Orth, Exposition Collectors and Historians Organization; Overlook Press; Michael Pender, World's Fair Collectors Society; Charles Silver, Museum of Modern Art Film Study Center; Eliot Sivowitch, Museum of History and Technology, Smithsonian Institution; Claire Stein and Theodora Morgan, National Sculpture Society; Theresa Turner, Teague Associates; Karel Yasko, General Services Administration.

Also: Henry Austin Clarke; Albert Cooper; Elaine de Kooning; Mrs. Alfred Joseph Dillon; Gordon W. Gilkey; Robert Ingle Hoyt, A.I.A.; Antoinette Kraushaar; Raymond Loewy; Jeffrey Meikle; Barbara Nicholls; George F. Pierrot; Doris Schleisner; Paul Shanley; George William Smith, A.I.A.; Donna Stein; Frederick Steiner; Wallace G. Teare, A.I.A.; Peter Wagner; Jerome Zerbe.

The public relations and press offices of several corporations which exhibited at the Fair, while not always able to supply the material for which we were searching, were consistently helpful and did their best to accommodate us. I wish especially to thank: John G. Agnello of General Motors; Frank Cogsville of Chrysler Corporation; Robert Henderson and Roy Morrow of Westinghouse; Robert Katzeff, Phyllis Moore, and Joseph Trachta of New York Telephone; Linda L. Lacher of American Express; M.L. Melville of NCR; Claire Paisner and Susan Holahan of Consolidated Edison; James Rebetta of General Electric; Robert C. Rogers of B.F. Goodrich; Adaline Ryan and Frank Sawyer of E.I. Du Pont de Nemours; John E. Sattler of Ford Motor Company; Robert Sharkey of Firestone; Frances Shoemaker of Heinz; Robert Shortal and Bob Niclas of RCA; James Sponseller of Fisher Body; Lee Whitehead of Greyhound; also, Arthur Schleifer of Restaurant Associates.

The staff of The Queens Museum has been unfailingly patient and helpful during the course of exhibition research. In particular, I wish to thank Janet Schneider, Executive Director, and Shelley Jane Grossberg, Assistant Director for Development, for their wholehearted support throughout the planning and implementation phases; Susan Lubowsky, Assistant Director for Programs, whose capable and energetic supervision of publications and promotion is deeply appreciated; and Deborah Silverfine, Film Curator/Education Assistant, who researched and organized the film program that accompanies the exhibition.

My assistant, Cynthia Kuchtuk, has coped with the myriad details concerning loans, cataloguing, and general organizational matters with admirable efficiency and stoicism. I thank her for her willing and capable help. Glenn Jones, on a student research project from the Urban School of San Francisco, and Eve Le Ber also gave a great deal of time and energy to helping us prepare catalogue material.

On a personal note, it remains for me to offer special thanks to my family—to my mother, Helen, and my husband, Roy Nicholson—without whose patience and loving support I should not have been able to devote myself to this project.

Helen A. Harrison
April, 1980

ome 300 yards south of The Queens Museum, surrounded by low stone benches in a circular copse of pines, a round granite marker identifies the site of two Time Capsules, both remnants of world's fairs. The earlier of these cylinders, with instructions that it be unearthed 5,000 years in the future, was assembled by the Westinghouse Corporation and·deposited on September 23, 1938 as a prelude to the great international exposition that was to open in Flushing Meadow the following spring.

Implicit in the depositing of the capsule was the hope that the American way of life would endure through the centuries until the day of disinterment arrived. Both tangibly and metaphorically the capsule symbolized the optimistic ideals that motivated the planners and sponsors of the 1939/1940 New York World's Fair—men and women who looked beyond the current climate of economic, social, and political distress to a future of peace and prosperity. This faith was also reflected in the theme they chose for the Fair: "Building the World of Tomorrow."

Like the capsule, the Fair represented a microcosmic view of civilization. It contained all the elements necessary to understand what its makers considered most valuable and memorable. To carry the analogy further, the Fair encapsulated the values and aspirations of a generation that had experienced an unprecedented crisis of confidence, had rummaged in the attic of its collective past for sources of strength and inspiration, and was now eager to embrace the concept of a future governed by material bounty and spiritual harmony. After ten years of the Great Depression, and with the sabers of war already rattling in Europe and the Orient, the Fair seemed to offer an alternative to both hardship and conflict. Its keynote was continuity through enlightened planning and development, seductively packaged in a fantasyland format, self-congratulatory and self-assertive—in short, just what we needed.

(AL)

Because the the Fair itself continues to occupy a major place in the popular imagination, our tendency has been to overlook the contradictions which surrounded it. From its inception in the spring of 1935, through its theoretical planning, development, construction, and final realization, the Fair was a vast and multifaceted undertaking. Although it occupied a slightly smaller area than the Louisiana Purchase Exposition of 1904, the World of Tomorrow was the most extensive and comprehensive of all international fairs. Held on the eve of a world war, it nevertheless attracted a larger contingent of official foreign exhibitors than any fair before or since. Yet attendance fell far short of the expected fifty million, and it ended up with an official deficit of nearly $19 million. Many of its predictions did not come true and we can now be amused by some of the enormous gaps in its futuristic formulations. The industries that dangled exciting new consumer goods before an eager public were obliged to abandon the production of their televisions, washing machines, and home air conditioners until after the war. Nations whose proud pavilions stood innocently side by side around the Court of Peace were actually either allying with or attacking one another in the real world outside. Even the Fair's two seasons were inconsistent, reflecting the changing world situation and the increasingly defensive posture the United States would take by 1940.

Perhaps most telling of all the contradictions was the Fair's ultimate compromise between theory and practice. Conceived as a demonstration of the triumph of enlightened social, economic, and technological engineering, it was in actuality a monument to merchandising, albeit in a rather more socially responsible guise than was to be seen again for many a decade. The Fair's ostensible message—that foresight and benevolent social guidance would result in a peaceful and prosperous future—was superseded by the more immediate marketing aims of American industry. The exhibits that made the strongest impact on the public imagination stressed the practical benefits of higher production, development, and growth over the theoretical potential for greater social good.

But in a magical world of captivating technological marvels and spectacular amusements, monumental architecture and extraordinary decoration, how many among us would have paused to contemplate the implications of these contradictions? True, there were those who criticized the Fair's motives and methods, who decried it as a façade of worthiness fronting for yet another mercantile extravaganza—and who saw Japan's rising sun in the dawn of that new day—but by and large people went to be amazed, amused, and distracted. That they also came away affected, educated—changed—was a function of both the Fair and the era which gave it meaning.

To complete the time capsule analogy, the current exhibition is a microcosm of the Fair itself; it offers a selection of all that was to be seen and experienced there, but it focuses on those aspects that in retrospect seem to have been the most telling. There is no doubt that both the exhibition and the catalogue merely begin to explore this fascinating and relatively untouched territory.

We have not intended a definitive analysis of the Fair. Instead, we hope the exhibition will stimulate reminiscence, and give cause for reflection, on the part of those who remember it and that it will provoke the curiosity and appreciation of those who do not. Let us consider this effort a beginning, just as its planners saw the Fair as the dawn of a new day.

Helen A. Harrison
Guest Curator

nvestigating the 1939/40 New York World's Fair offers an unusual perspective for viewing twentieth-century American culture. Accelerated by World War II, many of the artistic, social, and economic themes that came together there were to influence the shape of the second half of the century.

Much of the Fair's significance stems from its self-conscious effort to design a coherent model of American society that would accurately reflect its current condition and point the way to solutions for its most pressing problems. In undertaking this, the Fair developed a specific organizational structure which reflected its concept of future social requirements. It based its program on perceptions of the past shared by its designers and senior staff, and it drew its inspiration from a vision of the future derived from several major elements of the liberal past in America. In constructing its model of an "American Way of Life," the Fair drew upon the talents of many individuals whose intellectual and professional backgrounds were linked to the progressive tradition in America. The Fair's ultimate message was both strikingly prophetic and woefully short-sighted.

ORIGINS

The Fair's origins were in the New York business and financial community. In the spring of 1935 a group of civic-minded commercial leaders adopted the idea of sponsoring a world's fair as a means of alleviating some of the economic distress in the metropolitan area. They were encouraged in this enterprise by the popular and financial success of Chicago's "Century of Progress," which succeeded not only in attracting increased tourist business to the "windy city," but also managed to close its books showing a modest profit.

The New York effort was led by three influential members of the business community. George McAneny was president of the Title Guarantee and Trust Company and head of the Regional Planning Association. Grover Whalen, a former New York Police Commissioner, was president of Shenley Distilleries. Percy Straus was head of R.H. Macy's. In September 1935, these three were joined in incorporating the Fair by the heads of twenty-three banking and trust companies, thirty corporations, fifteen Wall Street law firms, eight insurance companies and retail firms, and eight business associations. (By contrast, there were only fifteen representatives from city, state, and national politics, eight individuals from the arts and education, and one labor leader.) Given this background, it was apparent that the Fair was expected to have a significant impact on the economic fortunes of the nation's largest city. It remained, however, for a different group to determine the content of the Fair and its significance in terms of social theory and cultural history.

Although public reaction to the Fair proposal was uniformly favorable, a dispute developed as to its appropriate design and theme. Contemporary journals described the conflict as one between the "traditionalist" and "functionalist" wings of the American art scene, and individuals and organizations began to take sides in the debate over the Fair's future.

Grover Whalen cheers at news of Howard Hughes's round-the-world flight in the plane, "New York World's Fair 1939," June 11, 1938. (PMW)

The "functionalists" were quick to seize the initiative. In December 1935, three months after the public incorporation of the Fair, the New York Civic Club was the site of a dinner party for "Progressives in the Arts." Organized by Michael Meredith Hare, secretary of the Municipal Art League, the effort was supported by architects Harvey Wiley Corbett and Ian Woodner-Silverman, industrial designers Gilbert Rohde and Walter Dorwin Teague, urban planner Henry Wright, and social commentator Lewis Mumford. At the dinner one hundred artists, designers, architects, and educators heard a series of speakers call for a new kind of Fair that would have relevance for contemporary social problems and that, in Mumford's words, would "project a pattern that will fulfill itself in the future of the whole civilization."

Mumford captured the tone of the gathering by criticizing past expositions for emphasis on technological advance divorced from social and historical significance. In his view, such a narrow perspective failed to grasp the real interrelationships within industrial civilization and inhibited a better understanding of how man could consciously alter his environment for the better.

Mumford summed up his theme for the evening in his opening address by predicting that:

> "The story we have to tell . . . and which will bring people from all over the world to New York, not merely from the United States, is the story of this planned environment, this planned industry, this planned civilization. If we can inject that notion as a basic notion of the Fair, if we can point it toward the future, toward something that is progressing and growing in every department of life and throughout civilization, not merely in the United States, not merely in New York City, but if we allow ourselves in a central position, as members of a great metropolis, to think for the world at large, we may lay the foundation for a pattern of life which would have an enormous impact in times to come."

THE FAIR OF THE FUTURE

An ad hoc group was formed to draft a more specific proposal for the Fair, based on the ideas put forth at the Civic Club. In addition to Hare and his initial circle of supporters, it included Louise Booney, N.H. Dearborn, Harvey Zorbaugh, Caleb Hornbostel, and Albert Mayer. Together they produced a detailed plan for what they called the "Fair of the Future." In it they argued that the Fair should be dedicated to the future of America and its unrealized opportunities for individual fulfillment and human progress. "Above all else," they emphasized, the fair "must stress the vastly increased opportunity and the developed mechanical means which this twentieth century has brought to the masses for better living and accompanying human happiness. Mere mechanical progress is no longer an adequate or practical theme for a World's Fair, we must demonstrate that supercivilization that is based on the swift work of machines, not on the arduous toil of men."

The proposal rejected what its authors considered the abstract and unnatural distinctions of past fairs, which attempted to deal with art, technology, and society in separate categories. Rather than simply extoll the virtues of machine civilization, the Fair would "examine the social consequences of these new processes and products." It would be organized in such a manner as to present a "unified whole which will represent all of the interrelated activities and interests of the American Way of Life."

To achieve these objectives the "Fair of the Future" Committee proposed new artistic, architectural, and exhibition techniques that would contribute to the overall plan and assist the Fair visitor to understand the exposition's central theme. In addition, the Fair corporation itself would construct a series of key exhibits highlighting the functions of modern living as well as a central-theme exhibit to provide an overview of the Fair's ideology. Finally, the Fair would establish guidelines for and exercise final approval over the exhibits of private companies to ensure that their displays contributed to the overall plan. "Both the Fair and Industry will be best served," the committee argued, "if industry adopts the strategy of emphasizing its place as a servant of man and demonstrates that it serves itself best by serving civilization."

To accomplish these goals, the committee recommended the creation of a Committee on Social Planning that would have responsibility for all aspects of the Fair's design and construction. Headed by a director of design and planning, the social planning committee would include representatives from architecture, industry, education, engineering, city planning, and public affairs and draw on the expertise of artists, sculptors, industrial designers, and landscape architects. If these proposals were adopted, the "Fair of the Future" Committee concluded, "For the first time in American history New York will represent to the world a vivid and integrated expression of the expanding American social scene, and by virtue of that expression alone will the World's Fair of 1939 achieve true architecture."[1]

Armed with this prospectus, the committee, along with a growing number of friends and supporters, convinced the business and financial leaders of the Fair corporation that its plan was the course to follow. The "Fair of the Future" proposal became the outline for the organization and theme of the Fair. Many of its key contributors and supporters worked at the Fair to implement their recommendations.

THE THEME COMMITTEE

Walter Dorwin Teague and Robert Kohn were directly responsible for translating the "Fair of the Future" into the 1939/40 New York World's Fair. Teague, a well-known member of the relatively young profession of industrial design, was a member of the "Fair of the Future" committee. His experience in exhibition technique gained at the Chicago and Dallas expositions was to play an important role at the Fair. In addition to being a member of the Fair's Board of Design and its Theme Committee,

Robert D. Kohn, Chairman of the Committee on Theme (cat. no. 7). (AL)

by intelligent coordinated effort for his community and for himself and will be able to realize the interdependence of every contributing form of life and work."[2]

The elements Teague and Kohn included as part of the Fair's theme provide a compendium of the intellectual history of progressive movements in the twentieth century. The overall concept was built upon the ideological foundations of more than four decades of American reform.

In approaching their task, the designers were concerned with three issues. First and most pressing was the economic dislocation caused by the Great Depression. The Fair's philosophy presumed that the means were at hand to provide abundance for all. The contradiction between this belief and the existence of economic want and material inequality was a major concern for Fair planners. The need for economic reform was closely related to a second issue: how to preserve democratic principles in the face of the challenge posed by fascism and communism. The planners saw a direct link between the material well-being of society and the strength of democratic institutions. The issues were perceived as aspects of an even more fundamental problem: the alienation of the individual from community. Thus, the effort to reintegrate man with his natural and social environment was the third and final major concern the Fair's designers had for the future of America.

Fair planners devised an ideology they believed would interpret the causes of contemporary economic distress, demonstrate the merits of democratic forms of government, and provide solutions for the problem of personal anomie in an industrial landscape. With the theme of "Building the World of Tomorrow," they attempted to construct a model of the future to address these issues by analyzing three categories of contemporary society. They began with an examination of the role of the machine in all aspects of human activity in relation to the concept of culture and, in particular, with respect to the ideas of cultural lag and national character. And they constructed a vision of the necessary components of the new community.

As a first step the Theme Committee divided the Fair into seven sectors designed to coincide with the major functional divisions of modern living: Production and Distribution; Transportation; Communications and Business Systems; Food; Medicine and Public Health; Science and Education; and Community Interests. Each sector was to have a central, or focal, exhibit to provide an overview of the sector's theme and to interpret the social significance of the displays of private companies in the same area. In addition, the Fair constructed a central theme exhibit in the Perisphere, to summarize the Fair's message and integrate the various focal exhibits.

In approaching the question of the machine and industrial civilization, Fair planners emphasized several key points, attempting to avoid the implication that either technology was responsible for society's ills or that it could resolve them. At the same time, they determined to demonstrate in new ways that the machine was the basic reality of modern society and that it had fundamentally altered human living conditions and created new modes of behavior and new standards for art and culture.

Teague received commissions from several major private exhibitors, including U.S. Steel and Ford. Kohn was past president of the American Institute of Architects, and—along with Lewis Mumford, Stuart Chase, Clarence Stein, and others—had been a founding member of the Regional Plan Association of America. He had served on the War Industries Board during World War I and had been head of the Housing Division of the Public Works Administration in the early days of the New Deal.

Teague, Kohn, landscape architect Gilmore Clarke, engineer R.H. Shreve, and architect Stephen Voorhees, comprised the Board of Design, which exercised overall supervisory powers. In addition, Teague and Kohn were the board's Theme Committee, directly responsible for devising the plan of the exposition. In their final report on theme, Kohn and Teague incorporated basic elements of the "Fair of the Future" proposal, emphasizing the need for a central message to demonstrate the interrelationship between technology and society and the potential for planned future change. The Fair was to "show the most promising developments of products, services and social factors of the present day in relation to their bearing on the life of the people. The American citizen will be able to see here what he could attain

Specifically, as technology had vastly increased the amount of time available for leisure, it had thus created the potential for a qualitative change in human relations and human activity. While this new-found leisure had freed man from many of the constraints of pre-industrial society, it had also created conditions which Fair planners believed increased the necessity for interdependence among all peoples if machines and their products were to be integrated into society.

THE FOCAL EXHIBITS

The Fair entrusted the development of its theme and focal exhibits to industrial designers, men believed to be in touch with the realities of the machine yet capable of speaking the public's language, of expressing new concepts of beauty and design. To Henry Dreyfuss, Raymond Loewy, Egmond Arens, Donald Deskey, Gilbert Rohde, Russell Wright, and George Sakier fell the task of translating the Fair's theme into concrete form.

In developing their plans, the designers worked closely with the Board of Design and the Theme Committee. In addition to Kohn and Teague, a number of other social planners were instrumental in tracing the outlines of the Fair's message. Michael Hare, secretary of the Fair of the Future Committee, served on the Board of Design for almost a year and participated in many of the early decisions on the nature of the Fair and its various exhibits. In answering the question, "Why have a Fair?," Hare traced the development of what he called a "producer's fair," designed to exchange technical information and increase trade. But improvements in communications and transportation had made such efforts meaningless. It was this very progress which posed the greatest threat to civilized life, he contended.

"The world is in chaos struggling to master its own inventions. We are in danger of being annihilated by forces which we ourselves set up. The world calls for an answer to this problem of mastering our own inventions *and we propose in 1939 to contribute to that answer.*"

Invoking George Washington and his inauguration, which the Fair officially celebrated, Hare called for a new beginning. In searching for a theme, he argued that "Today we are in a position *where we must master our inventions.*" Abandoning the producer's fair in favor of what he termed a "consumer's fair," Hare urged that the Fair not appeal "to the visitor as a technician in a particular field but rather . . . as an individual having needs and desires common to all people. . . . *Mere mechanical progress,*" he wrote, "*is no longer an adequate or practical theme for a world's fair.* Instead we must demonstrate an *American Way of Living.* We must tell the story of the relationships between objects in their everyday use—how they may be used and when purposefully used how they may help us."[3]

The Fair's efforts to portray these messages are best examined in the individual focal exhibits. The expression of its particular creator-designer, each at the same time embodied the Fair's concerns for the individual and society in an industrial world.

Gilbert Rohde, for example, expected to indicate in his Community Interests focal exhibit the social and cultural content of community life and the effects of technical change upon the activities of individuals and groups in society. The object of his exhibit, he wrote, was to show "the simplicity and coherence of elements in early community . . . [followed by] an increase in complexity and diversity and simultaneous disorganization . . . [leading eventually to] desired reorganization for richer environment."

In organizing his exhibit, Rohde proposed to draw a dichotomy between 1789 and 1939, the former characterized as "Man AND Community," the latter by "Man IN the Community." In the earlier period Rohde would demonstrate that life was based on a simple social organization in which men were relatively independent but were required to engage in heavy labor for most of their adult lives, leaving little time for leisure. It was the introduction of Science and Technology which transformed the colonial world into modern America. Man was required to organize these new forces and to create a whole range of communal government services. The result for modern man was a world in which he was freed from many burdensome chores, worked shorter hours, enjoyed better homes and cities, and had access to longer schooling and improved health. Rohde expected that the community of the future would engage in expanded adult education, develop a richer cultural life, patronize the arts, enjoy recreation, etc.

The details of the Community Interests exhibit are important today, not only because they shed light on the techniques of an industrial designer approaching a 1939 educational exhibit, but because they demonstrate the Fair's concern with technology in the making of the modern world. The community exhibit's action took place on a series of five sets. Set #1 was a representation of a colonial village green in 1789. A group of mechanical figures epitomized the life of the average man, a life composed, as the narrator emphasized, of "work, work, work," leaving little time for leisure or schooling. Rohde emphasized the

monotony of such an existence and stipulated that "a general atmosphere of dreariness" prevailed over these scenes of colonial conditions.

Sets #2 and #3 indicated with "kaleidoscope rapidity" the scientific and technical changes that had occured in the intervening 150 years. A circle about seven feet in diameter, equipped for rear projection, flashed before the spectator a succession of inventions which included the steam engine, the railroad, the telegraph, the phonograph, the automobile, the aeroplane, and the radio. This set's action took place within the larger background of Set #3, which consisted of a collection of wheels representing industry, commerce, and transportation. At the appropriate moment these wheels—a locomotive, ship propellor, gears in mesh, and truck tire—all began to spin, while a model of a generator glowed from the light of neon tubes. The dialogue noted that by 1939 these inventions had been applied by man to give him the power to speak, to move, and to make; it contrasted the first set's standard

Set 5, Community Interests focal exhibit: "Man Freed in Time and Space." (NYPL)

SET # 5 "MAN FREED IN TIME AND SPACE" EXHIBIT IN WALL 'A' - SCALE 1/4"=1'0"
TIME INDICATOR ALSO INCLUDED IN THIS SET, NOT SHOWN IN RENDERING.

COMMUNITY INTERESTS
FOCAL EXHIBIT
NEW YORK WORLDS FAIR
GILBERT ROHDE

5A

of sixteen hours of work and eight hours of sleep with the new world's "eight hours to produce, eight hours to play, to live, to enjoy the fruits of labor."

Set #4 added a touch of humor and concreteness. An animated figure, Mrs. Modern, was observed placing a series of telephone orders for all the possible attributes of a house, from its actual foundation to the contents of dinner, for delivery that afternoon. The division of labor had progressed to the point where one could acquire all of life's necessities by merely dialing the phone. This push-button society also demonstrated the theme of interdependence, since the action of Mrs. Modern required the involvement of thousands of people all over the world.

The final set posed Rohde's greatest challenge. Using a surrealistic model of man composed only of an eyeball, an ear, a nose, and a hand, Rohde animated the model to ascend from the base of the set to a position among the clouds. Each of these clouds concealed a different aspect of man's life now that he had been freed in space and time. Man's home as the central focus of his activities was illuminated and remained so throughout the action of the diorama. In the meantime, the various aspects of his new way of life were flashed behind the clouds. Newspapers, radio, sports, hobbies, travel, movies, fine arts, and schools were intended to portray the inhabitant of 1939 as vitally involved in and informed about the world around him. A final scene showed the context in which the new man was expected to operate, a modern housing

Donald Deskey's design for the Communications focal exhibit. (AL)

project representing his restored sense of community. As the lights faded on this last scene, the narrator echoed the obvious conclusion:

"Time for interest in government, in community, in the group. Time to plan for our community. At last Man is freed . . . freed in time and space." As the last light faded out on the final set, a spotlight switched on, illuminating the enigmatic words, "For what?"[4]

Raymond Loewy's focal exhibit for the Transportation zone was less sweeping in its message. Although Teague and Hare had expressed early on in planning documents the hope that the exhibit would concentrate on the effects of new highway systems and their implications for rural/urban contact, the actual display consisted of a large map that demonstrated with lights the distance a person could travel in one day via various modes of transportation. This demonstration of improved machinery concluded with a highly dramatic, but from Fair planners' viewpoint, socially irrelevant, rocket trip to London.[5]

The Communications exhibit by Donald Deskey also lacked some of the social implications of Rohde's work. Although Deskey agreed with Teague's prospectus, which emphasized communications' role as the nervous system of modern society, he confined his actual exhibit to a symbolic representation of its importance in contemporary life. Man was depicted by a twenty-foot tall transparent, plastic head. As Man spoke, the symbols of seven instruments of communication materialized on a plastic disk in front of him, and their images were projected on a thirty-foot plastic globe suspended at the opposite end of the exhibit hall. The seven means of communication were postal service, the printed word, telegraph, telephone, motion picture, radio, and television.[6]

The Food exhibit by Russell Wright involved considerable cooperation of personnel from the U.S. Department of Agriculture. Its over-all message, in the designer's words, was to present a "picture of the great coherent organization of materials and forces which relieve man of the necessity of giving all his living hours to the task of cultivating and raising food to sustain only that very life which he is giving to the task." Wright's contention was that "nutrition is the key to leisure and freedom, to time for science, art, learning, and entertainment."

If it was also somewhat bizarre, Wright's was certainly the most entertaining and imaginative of all the focal exhibits. In a room whose floor, walls, and ceilings were all painted dark red, Wright placed a series of giant white monoliths of varying shapes and sizes. Each contained a different exhibition demonstrating some aspect of the Miracle of Food. A cut-out figure representing man transformed its flesh first into the chemical compounds from which it was made and then into the foods from which man obtained his essential chemical requirements. An overhead sign duly informed the Fair visitor that "Man = Chemicals = Food." An aerial view of New York, complete with three-dimensional models of the Chrysler and Empire State buildings, included, for comparison's sake, mounds of food depicting the yearly needs of 130,000,000 Americans. Other displays illustrated the ways

Model of Raymond Loewy's "Rocketport," Transportation focal exhibit. (PMW)

agricultural labor had been altered in the modern world; the improvements made in new strains of plants; the advances in pesticide control; the restoration of land through fertilization, crop control, irrigation, and erosion control; new discoveries in chemical farming, processing, and packaging; and the importance of transportation in diversifying the food supply and alleviating local famine.

The demonstration of these admittedly academic facts took place within the monoliths and involved such devices as a cauliflower equipped with a boxing glove to K.O. a giant winged monster—pest control—and a field in the form of a face, which alternately smiled or frowned, depending upon the amount of restoration to which it had been exposed. Undoubtedly the most unusual scene appeared in the last set, a giant 60-foot egg. Here the spectator was confronted by: an avocado, five jewels glowing from its skin, climbing a mountain peak; a flight of lobsters winging its way into the interior; a trans-Atlantic aqueduct spilling roses into the desert; an eye blinking mysteriously from a cave; and a clock inside a can racing madly backwards. The meaning of this surrealistic landscape was conveyed to the uninitiated by the ever present narrator, who explained that the avocado's jewels stood for the five nutritional elements found in food, the lobsters for modern transportation, the blinking eye for man's victory over night blindness through vitamin A, the clock running backwards for the benefits of modern canning, and the aqueduct for irrigation.[7]

The display that involved some of the greatest effort, and that underwent the greatest changes from conception to finished design, was Egmond Arens's Production and Distribution focal exhibit. After months of debate and the involvement of many Fair staff members and several public and private consultants, the Fair formulated a basic program for the sector. "It is important to emphasize," they wrote, "that it is the concerted effort of millions of people that makes mass production possible, and that mass production ties people together in a net from which there is no possible escape . . . . If the exhibit as a whole can be planned to carry one broad message in addition to the story of interrelationships, that message should be that production and consumption are equal . . . . It leads to the further statement that any proposal for economic action must be judged in the end by its effects on total production."

On a large curved screen, Arens portrayed the number of activities which went into filling a single grocery order. Using film and still shots, the display pictured Mrs. Jones ordering spare ribs; this was followed by scenes of cowboys, herders, tradesmen, stockyard workers, trainmen, etc.—all working to produce the goods and services required.

Below this overall representation of interdependence, Arens included three subsidiary exhibits. The first, Man's Heritage of Power, was a demonstration of the development of machine power, contrasting what it termed the Dark Ages of Scarcity with the New Age of Abundance. The second section addressed the contradictions between abundance and economic inequality.

Arens constructed eight boxes to represent eight categories of a family's expenses: education, health, clothing, housing, household, food, travel, and recreation. Above the boxes was a graph with four sets of lines representing different levels of family spending. The levels, drawn from Department of Agriculture and WPA studies, were divided among a subsistence level of $800/year, a maintenance level of $2,000/year, the good life minimum of $2,500/year, and a luxury minimum of $5,000 and over. The exhibit reported that one-third of the nation's families earned less than the subsistence level and fully nine-tenths received less than $2,500, the minimum for the good life. As the visitor pushed the buttons under each box, pictures appeared portraying different life styles in each expenditure category. At the same time, a light would rise above the box, indicating the level of income required to sustain that standard of living.

Arens added the obvious conclusion: "As mass production depends upon mass purchasing power, we cannot hope to build lasting prosperity under such conditions of inadequate purchasing power." "One hundred and fifty years ago," the designer observed, "the proposal to raise the incomes of the entire population to the Good Life minimum would have been considered impossible. With modern technology and power production it is no longer physically impossible. We have the techniques and the power to produce abundance; we need now to discover a workable formula for its distribution to 'Three-Thirds of a Nation'."

In the final section of the exhibit, Arens contrasted "Yesterday, Today and Tomorrow." A series of statements flashed before the visitor posed the following dilemmas:

In George Washington's time most people led isolated lives.
Today men cooperate readily with each other for physical needs.
Will cooperation also include human understanding?

Sources of information were unreliable, knowledge limited and haphazard.
Network of communications systems makes for speedy exchange of ideas.
Can we improve the spiritual side of life as we did the physical apparatus?

Other sets of statements raised issues such as:

Can serious breakdowns be avoided in such a complex system?
Will atomic power liberate gigantic new forces for man's use?
Will increased leisure bring political and cultural renaissance?

The final set proclaimed that:

A better world for all was the Founding Fathers' dream. Will it come true?
We already have the technique, if not the body, of abundance for all. Let's go.
Resolved: that new techniques shall solve human problems in the World of Tomorrow.[8]

CULTURE AND ALIENATION

Despite Arens's conclusion, the Fair's theme did not expect technical advance to solve the problems besetting modern society. Before they were prepared to describe the characteristics of the World of Tomorrow, Fair planners concentrated their attention on the role of culture in shaping human behavior.

Culture, to Fair planners, was a multidimensional concept derived from at least three distinct movements in American intellectual history. All three shared a common heritage in the work of sociologist William Ogburn, who had invented the concept of cultural lag in the early twenties. Ogburn contended that various elements in society change at different rates, and that such disparities were fundamentally responsible for the tensions of human societies. It was the peculiar characteristic of modern societies that their technical or material bases were changing more rapidly than their adaptive or cultural dimensions. The seeming inability of moral values, economic theory, political institutions, and artistic standards to keep pace with technological innovation was the root cause of many of the difficulties faced by industrial societies. What was needed, Ogburn proposed, was a concerted and conscious effort on the part of society as a whole to anticipate technical change and to plan for its incorporation into the community by adjusting the cultural base.

With culture as a major focus of social analysis and cultural lag, with respect to technology, as the key to modern society, three related efforts were made to explore American society, all of which were instrumental in shaping the theme of the Fair.

In the field of anthropology, Margaret Mead and Ruth Benedict were among the prominent social scientists who applied the tool of cultural analysis to their work among primitive people and related it to issues in modern American society. Their studies of Zuni Indians and South Seas islanders repeatedly emphasized the relationship between a society's cultural configuration and its overall mental and spiritual well-being. While their studies were not efforts to evaluate the relative worth of one civilization over another, they consistently compared their findings with the problems confronting twentieth-century America. In so doing, they stressed the importance of cultural patterns—rather than biological inheritance, political institutions, or economic relationships—as the primary means of understanding social issues.[9]

The significance of culture as the determining agent in social relations was shown by a second application of the concept of cultural lag applied to contemporary problems.

In their studies of "Middletown," Robert and Helen Lynd consciously sought to apply anthropological techniques to their investigations of Muncie, Indiana. Subtitling their works "A Study in Modern American Culture" (1929) and "A Study in Cultural Conflict" (1937), the Lynds concluded that this "typical" American community suffered from a fundamental malaise that could be traced to the failure of its system of values and beliefs to keep pace with the technological changes that had affected its everyday life. These changes had had an impact on every aspect of social intercourse in Middletown, including family and personal relations, individual and communal leisure activity, working conditions, and political debates. From the Lynds' point of view, what accounted for the disruptions behind Middletown's seemingly placid façade was, in every instance, the inability of the community to adjust its attitudes toward work, play, education, and the family as quickly as it assimilated new machines and new products.

The Lynds were forced to conclude that "in view of the rapidity of some cultural changes in Middletown in recent decades, its resistance to change, its failure to embrace change as an opportunity to lessen its frictions, may constitute a liability to its own values."[10]

While Mead and Benedict were exploring the details of primitive cultures and the Lynds were investigating darkest Indiana, a third approach to the concept of culture was manifesting itself in the search for a uniquely American culture that would integrate its best traditions with its machine environment. This search for a "usable past" was most evident in the work of Van Wyck Brooks, Lewis Mumford, and Constance Rourke as they sought to find in American experience models upon which to construct a new cultural tradition and to define a distinctive American character. Their efforts involved reevaluation of American literature, folklore, art, music, and architecture and began by rejecting as artificial attempts to interpose European or classical standards onto an American setting. What Lewis Mumford termed "The Imperial Façade" applied not only to the construction of railroad stations and country homes modeled after Greek and Roman temples but to the whole constellation of efforts to impose what he regarded as outmoded canons of truth and beauty on the instruments and organization of a machine civilization.[11]

The search for a "usable experience" concentrated on those instances in the American experience which were considered unique. The writings of Walt Whitman, the architecture of H.H. Richardson and Frank Lloyd Wright, the parks of Frederick Law Olmstead, the paintings of Thomas Eakins, and the photography of Alfred Steiglitz—all were cited as examples of a new cultural tradition, in harmony with its environment and properly adapted to conditions of modern life.

These three elements—the importance of culture as a tool of social analysis, the application of the idea of cultural lag to explain the dysfunctions of American society, and the search for a national cultural identity—were all expressed by the Fair. Mumford, in his earliest remarks to the Committee, had predicted that "what will be projected at the Fair [will be] the new school, the new theater, the new museum, the new playground, the new community." The Fair of the Future report itself predicted that art and architecture at the Fair and in the nation would "evolve as an expression of our unique social order," and that the Fair, with its coordinated central theme, would provide a forum for the creation of new cultural patterns compatible with the machine civilization of twentieth-century America.

Expression of the Fair's cultural theme took many forms, including its commitment to a functional architecture, its emphasis on the coherent planning of the Fairgrounds as part of an over-all park design, its sculpture and mural programs, and the inclusion in every focal exhibit of a sense of the relationship between technology and new forms of artistic expression and communal living.

INDUSTRIAL DESIGN AS THE MODEL FOR CHANGE

Teague related the Fair's interest in pre-industrial cultures, industrial design, urban planning, and political institutions in his book on the Fair, *Design This Day*. Citing Franz Boas, Teague noted that the slovenly workmanship so common in industrial society was unknown in peasant communities, and he described this "instinct for workmanship" as a fundamental characteristic of coherent cultures. Appealing to the American example set by the colonial villagers and Shaker craftspeople, Teague argued that the skills of industrial design be used in shaping the total environment. Failure to apply the principles of order and harmony would have consequences far beyond questions of esthetics. Equating lack of design and planning with the failure of the democratic ideal, he warned that "our Hamtracks, Ciceros, and Long Island Cities stem from the same source that, in another phase, have produced Nazi and fascist ideologies and communist autocracies."[12]

In contrast to this potential disaster, Teague and other Fair planners were convinced of the efficacy of their model for the future.

"A common motive, shared ideals, inclinations and preferences held by many men alike with the means to give them effect—these are the necessary preliminaries to the reconstruction of a satisfactory scheme of living."

Art and society and technology and culture were inseparable aspects of the same equation, and a viable culture would depend on the restructuring of the social order if they were to be reformed.[13]

From the Fair planners' point of view, the elements for creating a new culture and designing an American way of life were already visible. The forms of modern aircraft, the construction of parkways and bridges, the shape of domestic and office appliances, experiments in housing and regional planning were all manifestations of the search for an American culture—a search that characterized much of the thirties and formed part of the basis for the Fair's ideology. Teague contended that industrial designers were:

> Exploring that exact unity which machine precision establishes as the ideal end of our creative efforts. One thing we are confident we know about this world we hope to build, and that is that it will be free from the confusions, wastes, and frustrations that we can see all around us today. In its small and great elements, and in its dominating scheme, we believe it will have a serene harmony and a smoothly functioning unobtrusive organization which will give the individual full scope to exercise whatever capacity for enjoyment of life and for fruitful activity he possesses. It will have the perfect integration of parts we see today in some of our products that machine production makes possible.[14]

From this perspective of the role of technology and culture in contemporary society, Fair planners were prepared to build a model of the World of Tomorrow that would detail the elements of the future shape of society. They outlined a process of education, recognized the crucial role of science, and examined the functions of home and family, in order to design a model of urban and regional planning incorporating their thinking. They continued to emphasize the machine as the motive force in social change and culture as the principle mechanism for adapting to it.

ADAPTATION BY EDUCATION

From the Fair planners' viewpoint, education was a continuing process of adaptation rather than the transmission of a set of truths. The individual would learn how to interpret the world around him and understand the forces operating in society. Donald Slesinger, designer of the Fair's education exhibit, described education as an "intellectual safeguard for the individual against the confusions, maladjustments, and misconceptions of a changing civilization." Education was a functional tool to prepare the individual for his or her responsibilities in a changing world and to qualify the citizen for his or her part in a democratic society.

In describing the objectives of education, Fair designers maintained that science would play a central role. For them, science did not represent either the products created by new technologies nor the laws derived from the biological or physical universes. Rather, science implied a particular way of looking at both individual and social experience. Gerald Wendt, science director of the Fair and author of *Science in the World of Tomorrow* (1939), believed that science was best understood as a method and spirit rather than a body of knowledge or collection of products.

Wendt, whose broad experience spanned the academic and business communities, viewed the research spirit as an almost primal instinct and saw the research method as an essential mechanism for examining the problems of contemporary society. This approach, he argued, was divorced from ideological considerations and transcended outmoded systems of belief. What was needed in considering educational requirements in the future, Wendt believed, was a spirit of scientific curiosity and a willingness to apply the scientific method to social problems. "The ambitions of women, the disintegration of the home, the liberalizing of education, respectability of divorce, the unrestrained dreams of youth, the decline of the church, are all facts not accounted for in our inherited culture."[15] Stripped of cultural and ideological preconceptions, Wendt believed the average citizen would inevitably come to the conclusion that the advance of industrial civilization had had two major social effects: an increase in the degree of individual freedom with respect to one's personal life and a corresponding increase in the degree of interdependence in economic relationships.

As the Fair planners were outlinling the future functions of education and science, they were preparing to depict some details of life in the World of Tomorrow. They were particularly concerned about the home and the familial relations of those who would live in it.

THE SHAPE OF THINGS TO COME

To Fair planners, a home was not just a house. It was a demonstration of the impact of technology on the most mundane aspects of human behavior; it contributed to the definition of a new American culture adapted to the machine world. New types of functions and appliances were essential parts of a larger whole and would be displayed, one Fair planner proclaimed, "as distinctive elements of an organic unity whose completeness is essential to their significance and charm."

The new home would be more democratic, since the functions of servants would be taken over by new appliances available to a wider section of the population. These products also would express the machine ethic which the Fair considered fundamental to modern living. Because machine production was uniform in quality and design, it would provide a new basis for democratic equality. The planners believed that the purchase and use of new appliances and furnishings were not simply a matter of economic necessity but fundamentally related to the larger effort to define a uniquely American character. "One of the finest examples," wrote Mumford, "not merely of utilitarian accomplishment but of esthetic impulse, is the modern American kitchen . . . ." Wendt echoed this assessment by concluding that "the mass production methods of American industry, operating with inexpensive materials, have long made the American bathroom synonymous with American civilization."[16]

The Fair's perception of the home and its various physical components was linked to its view of the family as a consumer unit. As Egmond Arens had sought to demonstrate with his production and distribution exhibit, the primary issue for American society was to increase purchasing power to allow larger portions of the population to consume the goods and services that defined American life. An American way of life was conceived in terms of individual ability to consume larger and larger quantities of material objects, not simply because of the positive impact on economic conditions, but because this behavior was an expression of confidence in the very nature of machine civilization, and because the products themselves represented a basic element of the American character.

Wendt was prepared to predict a number of specific changes that would accompany the acceptance of increased leisure and expanded buying power. For example, there would be an increase in the time and energy devoted to all forms of physical activity. New service industries would arise to satisfy the demand for recreation, although Wendt also predicted a decline in interest in professional sports.

There would be a new interest in a wide range of cultural and artistic activities, both in terms of comsumption and creation. "Gardening, building, woodworking, sculpture and painting, music, photography, and science" would all be growth industries, filling the leisure time that would characterize the World of Tomorrow.

Robot demonstration, Westinghouse exhibit, 1940. (PMW)

All of these activities were regarded not merely as expressions of individual taste, but as reflections of a fundamental human instinct for creative activity—an instinct that industrial civilization had now freed from the necessity for arduous labor for the sake of subsistence. This new curiosity would form the basis for what Wendt described as true culture.

THE CITY AND THE REGION

The Fair's vision of the home and family were aspects of still another model of the future that encompassed a larger field of view. The city, the region, and the nation as a whole were to be made over as part of the effort to create a national character in harmony with its industrial base. The demands of technology, most especially the needs of the automobile, required a new approach to urban design and regional planning. Vast new construction projects were needed to link urban and rural areas into new kinds of communities.

Again it was Gerald Wendt who captured the significance of the automobile for the American character.

Americans live in their cars. Here they attain temporary privacy, an isolation from pressing neighbors. Here they enjoy the sensation of motion, of action and progress, even though it be vicarious and futile. Here they feel too the sense of power and of control over their course and destiny which is otherwise lost in their dependence on society. Here they escape from monotony and often from squalor. Thus the American nation has become mobile, optimistic, and occupied with external change of scene rather than with stability and the improvement of their permanent conditions of living.[17]

Despite Wendt's distaste for some of the automobile's effects on the American character, his analysis was more than justified by the tremendous reception given to Norman Bel Geddes's Futurama exhibit for General Motors. Vast panoramas depicted the construction of a massive interstate highway system characterized by multilaned, limited-access roads, giant interchanges, and graceful suspension bridges. Though Bel Geddes's exhibit lacked some of the more subtle elements of the Fair's central theme, it was the most successful (and popular) statement of the future shape of the American landscape.

DEMOCRACITY

The ultimate expression of the Fair's message was the Theme Center, found in the central exhibit that had been the touchstone of the Fair's planning from the earliest drafts. Architecturally, visually, and symbolically at the center of the Fair, the Trylon and Perisphere were meant to sum up all of the interrelated elements of the Fair's theme. Designed by Wallace K. Harrison and J. André Foulihoux, who had recently collaborated with other firms on Rockefeller Center, the Trylon and Perisphere were not intended to compete with New York's skyscrapers, but to epitomize their contribution to modern civilization. In keeping with the canons of industrial design, both were conceived as pure forms devoid of unnecessary adornment as well as functional structures designed to serve as exhibit spaces and central images.

The interior of the Perisphere was the fullest expression of the Fair's ideology. Inside the great globe, industrial designer Henry Dreyfuss constructed Democracity, a model that was to represent the basic ideals of the World of Tomorrow.

Democracity was designed as the perfectly planned community of the future. In a single statement, it incorporated all the social and cultural ideas of the Fair's design. The model that Dreyfuss constructed represented an area of 11,000 square miles and contained a theoretical population of 1.5 million people. The

First preview of Perisphere interior, April 27, 1939. (FC)

region was divided into several subdivisions; Centerton was the business, educational, social, and cultural hub which included a nine-to-five population of 250,000. As the recorded narration of H.V. Kaltenborn pointed out, however, most of this population commuted between their jobs and the approximately seventy satellite towns surrounding Centerton. These suburbs were carefully planned communities designed for modern living.

Pleasantvilles with populations of 10,000 were exclusively residential in nature, while Millvilles of 25,000 contained light industry as well as bedroom communities. Between the Pleasantvilles, Millvilles, and Centerton were large greenbelt areas consisting of both agricultural land and recreational parks.

Linking the various elements of Democracity were modern express highways and parkways that were not only efficient means of transportation but visible expressions of machine design as well as a functional method of linking communities with their usable past. Using this network of transportation, families could expend their leisure time by exploring the historic preserves and natural areas that would contribute to the definition of a native American culture.[18]

In an image typical of the thirties, power for Democracity was provided by a giant hydroelectric plant located on the river that conveniently ran through the region. This version of the TVA enabled Fair planners to prophesy a pollution-free environment in the World of Tomorrow.

Robert Kohn, board of design chairman, predicted that:

This is not a vague dream of a life that might be lived in the far future but one that could be lived tomorrow morning if we willed it so. The great, crushing, all absorbing city of today . . . would no longer be a planless jumble of slum and chimney, built only for gain, but an effective instrument for human activities, to be used for the building of a better world of tomorrow. . . . The relation between these units of stone and steel, highway and green is a symbol of the new life of tomorrow; that life will be based on an understanding of the contribution of all elements to a new and living democracy.

BEYOND THE WORLD OF TOMORROW

The Fair, bringing its message of peace and unity, ironically was opened on the eve of the 20th-century's second massive effort at self-destruction. When the smoke and tumult of that cataclysm finally lifted, the ideals and images that made up the model of Democracity would, in fact, take concrete form, but seldom in the configurations or with the consequences Fair planners had predicted.

The Full Employment Act of 1948 capped the process whereby the federal government accepted responsibility for maintaining levels of income and, by definition, levels of consumption required by an expanding economy. Designers increasingly were employed by industry to shape and reshape their products, but the esthetic philosophies espoused at the Fair were soon forgotten in the process of competition. The automobile became firmly entrenched as the symbol of American culture and the possession of one or two by every family an expression of democratic equality. Its use for a new array of leisure activities was facilitated by the construction of a network of interstate highways that provided access between urban and rural areas and gave rise to a new type of community—the suburb.

The acceptance of and demand for domestic appliances exceeded expectations, and "Better living through Chemistry" became a hallmark of American life. But rather than moving toward a modern, native design for family dwellings, postwar Americans seemed determined to experiment with a variety of identities, living in homes copied from colonial, Spanish, or Tudor motifs and furnished accordingly.

Rather than being located in carefully planned suburban communities with access to recreational opportunities, America's postwar homes were crowded into vast tract developments with little thought for preserving aspects of the natural environment or providing an infrastructure for human needs. Center cities were abandoned to those segments of the population that were still economically or socially deprived, and the urban infrastructure—transit, schools, parks—was left to strangle on a declining economic base.

The effort to identify and define an American Way of Life was, in a Cold War environment, translated into an attack against Un-American activities. The most prominent descendant of the Trylon and Perisphere was a pentagon.

America and New York had succeeded in becoming the art and architecture capital of the world and modernism had triumphed as the new standard of esthetics. But rather than unifying culture, art seemed to become preoccupied with individual visions increasingly divorced from the understanding and support of the general population.

The designers of the World of Tomorrow had attempted to construct a model of the future based on their perceptions of future contemporary society. They foresaw a new community that would be adaptive to its changing material base, that would emphasize the distribution of new devices and objects as expressions of a fundamental equality, and that would adopt new aesthetic standards based on a common cultural heritage.

Insofar as they failed to confront issues of power within American society and ignored mechanisms for political change, their vision was doomed to failure. At the same time, their efforts cannot simply be dismissed as naïve efforts to predict the future; their insights into the potential changes in American life still have profound relevance and their over-all exploration of the relationship between industrial civilization, political freedom, and individual fulfillment still constitutes a significant achievement. Their utilization of the concept of culture and their search for an American past that would be relevant to the present have added materially to our understanding of society and may yet point the way toward a new world. Their challenge—to define a society that balanced the demands of individual expression with the search for unifying communal goals—remains unmet.

NOTES:

One of the delights of working on the 1939/40 New York World's Fair is to encounter the organization's sense of historic importance. This led it to create an enormous file of information and material, carefully indexed, which is now located in the Manuscripts and Archives Division of the New York Public Library. Rather than attempt to provide detailed footnotes for all references and quotes in the text, these brief notes will simply designate the appropriate files in the Fair's archives from which material was taken. Where specific documents have titles and dates, these are included.

1. NYWF Archives C 1.0, Fair of the Future. NYWF Archives PR 1.41, Address by Lewis Mumford, 12/11/35.

2. NYWF Archives A 1.13, Report of the Theme Committee, 7/16/36.

3. NYWF Archives PR 1.41, "Why Have a Fair?," Michael Hare, 12/22/36.

4. NYWF Archives C 1.02, Community Interests Focal Exhibit.

5. NYWF Archives C 1.02, Transportation Focal Exhibit.

6. NYWF Archives C 1.02, Communications Focal Exhibit.

7. NYWF Archives C 1.02, Food Focal Exhibit.

8. NYWF Archives C 1.02, Production and Distribution Focal Exhibit.

9. Ruth Benedict, *Patterns of Culture* (1934). Margaret Mead, *Growing up in New Guinea* (1930). *Coming of Age in Samoa* (1928).

10. Robert and Helen Lynd, *Middletown: A Study in Modern American Culture* (1929). *Middletown in Transition: A Study in Cultural Conflict* (1937).

11. Constance Rourke, *American Humor* (1931). Lewis Mumford, *Stick and Stones* (1924). *The Golden Day* (1926). *The Brown Decades* (1931).

12. NYWF Archives C 2.504, "Industrial Art and Its Future," Walter Dorwin Teague, 11/18/36.

13. Walter Dorwin Teague, *Design This Day* (1940).

14. "Industrial Art and Its Future "

15. Gerald Wendt, *Science in the World of Tomorrow* (1939).

16. Lewis Mumford, *The Culture of Cities* (1938). Gerald Wendt, *Science in the World of Tomorrow* (1939).

17. NYWF Archives PR 1.41, Address by Gerald Wendt, 7/5/39.

18. NYWF Archives C 1.0, Theme Building, Democracity.

Joseph P. Cusker, who specializes in contemporary American history, is Executive Director of the New England Land Grant Universities.

THE PEOPLE'S FAIR:
Cultural Contradictions of a Consumer Society

Warren I. Susman

n 1935 the American critic Kenneth Burke addressed the first of three American Writers' Congresses on the theme Revolutionary Symbolism in America. His intention was to convince the largely pro-communist audience of the importance of myths as social tools for welding effective interrelationships and for forging the organization to achieve common ends. The particular myth for which he pleaded, the positive symbol for which he called, was that of "the people."

> In suggesting that "the people," rather than "the worker," rate highest in our hierarchy of symbols . . . I am suggesting fundamentally that one cannot extend the doctrine of revolutionary thought among the lower middle class without using middle-class values . . . The symbol of "the people," . . . also has the tactical advantage of pointing more definitely in the direction of unity. . . . It contains the ideal, the ultimate classless feature which the revolution would bring about—and for this reason seems richer as a symbol of allegiance. It can borrow the advantages of nationalistic conditioning and at the same time be used to combat the forces that hide their class prerogatives behind a communal ideology.

"We convince a man by reason of the values we and he hold in common," said Burke, and in fact the idea of the people was basic to American folkways.

We do not know whether the critic convinced his audience. We do know—any reading of the culture of the 1930s affirms it—that the idea of the people is in abundant evidence in the rhetoric of the period, a fundamental image that appeared to speak deeply of the American consciousness.

Because the rhetoric of an era often betrays the real—if often obscured—issues about the nature of a culture, it deserves serious examination. Certainly during the period from 1935 until the end of World War II, there was one phrase, one sentiment, one special call on the emotions that appeared everywhere in America's popular language: the people. It was not a new rhetorical flourish, to be sure, but the 1930s would see it acquire new functions. Never very precise as an ideological concept, it was now used to summon up notable outpourings of feelings to provide—somehow—an emotional base for an entire nation. With the birth of the so-called Popular Front in Western Europe, as well as in the United States, the people was a term meant to cut through divisions of class, ethnicity, and ideological distinctions of left and right to form a basic sentiment on which a national culture might be founded.

Thus Carl Sandburg gave us "The People, Yes"; The W.P.A. projects offered Art for the People and The People's Theater; Frank Capra provided a series of enormously successful populist films in praise of "the little man"; and John Ford, most significantly in a number of films made near the end of the 1930s, rewrote American history in mythic and populist terms. And, while no

A. Meyer and Lill forming a Trylon and Perisphere, on the site of the demolished Theme Center. (PMW)

17

statistical account is available, one might guess that more members of the audience responded tearfully than not to the image of Jane Darwell, playing Steinbeck's Ma Joad in Ford's film version of *The Grapes of Wrath*, when she delivered the final defiant speech with which the work closes: "We're the people that live. Can't nobody wipe us out. Can't nobody lick us. We'll go on forever. We're the people." Miss Darwell won a 1940 Academy Award for her performance. It was the heyday of the people.

The primary usefulness of this idea in the late 1930s was its ability to suggest that a basic unity underpinned the whole social and cultural structure of America. Divisions within society seemed superficial. Somehow, if they could only be allowed to talk or be instructed in what to say, the people could easily speak out in one voice. Perhaps because there seemed to be so many things that did divide, the idea of unity seemed crucial. A search was launched for some method of measuring and defining this unity and therefore of dealing with it properly. Statistics might very well prove the key. The concept of the average was born, a kind of statistical accounting of the people seen as a unit. For a culture that originally had enshrined individualism as its key virtue, interest in the average was now overweening. The Average American and the Average American Family became central to the new vision of a future culture. And by the 1930s additional statistical facts could be added to complete the picture of the average American: Public opinion polls, from techniques developed in the mid-1930s, provided "scientific" evidence about thoughts and attitudes. Increasingly, this statistical creature—the average American—became central to cultural thinking and planning. He or she was soon invested as well with the sentimental aura that went with the more mystical notion of the people. If the people seemed pleasingly poetic and the average American suitably scientific, both versions of the idea nevertheless regarded society as a single entity. And both of these notions are essential to any serious assessment of American culture in the 1930s.

America's nineteenth-century seer, Ralph Waldo Emerson, once insisted about his countrymen, "We want our Dreams and our Mathematics." Frequently these are but two sides of the same coin, such as the people, and the average American. The New York World's Fair of 1939/1940 pinched that coin and pinched it hard. It insisted it was the People's Fair and developed itself for the average American. The very appeal it sought, and gained, revealed basic contradictions that were crucial not only to the history of the Fair but to the culture from which it came.

Perhaps that was inevitable, for the Fair, almost as if it were consciously heeding Emerson's words, simultaneously demanded both Dreams and Mathematics. From the outset its ideological Dreams would be battering against the harsher realities of its Mathematics, its desire to please an America of consumers. This conflict was to pervade its history.

When the corporation that built the Fair ceased to be in 1945, it did an unusual thing: it left a small sum of money to commission the writing and publication of the Fair's history, "useful to those charged with organizing and operating future exhibitions." That little volume, *Making a World's Fair*, primarily

North parking lot, on the present site of Shea Stadium. (NYP)

was based on the sixteen volumes of the minutes of the meetings of its board of directors. Written by a business reporter, Ed Tyng, it was not published until 1958, by a vanity press. It remains virtually unknown, and there is little evidence that it was, in fact, of value to anyone who was responsible for later fairs. But *Making . . .* is remarkably fruitful for the historian who wishes to understand how the Fair-makers saw their own achievement, and especially how they understood the idea of the people and the average American, so central to their thought and rhetoric.

In his introduction to the book, Grover A. Whalen, the Fair's president, recalled that "The Fair was built for and dedicated to the people. It was built to delight and instruct them."

for "the plain American citizen."

No previous Fair, neither European or American, had developed such a rhetoric of popular concern, a rhetoric so closely in keeping with the idiom from which it had sprung. Previous Fairs had shared what Whalen argued in his introduction was the demonstration of "the best industrial techniques, social ideas and services, the most advanced scientific discoveries of its day." But none had so openly articulated a message or lesson for the people. Again in Whalen's words, the Fair "conveyed the picture of the interdependence of man on man, class on class, nation on nation. It attempted to tell of the immediate necessity of enlightened and harmonious cooperation to preserve and save the best of modern civilization as it was then known."

Notice how significantly the rhetoric relates to the general concept of the people previously mentioned. The stress on unity, cooperation, interdependence, harmony—all relate in important ways to a general idea of the people. And while Fair literature contained much talk about the future—the World of Tomorrow—there was also considerable emphasis on *saving* "the best of modern civilization as it was then known."

All fairs may be said to educate but this one insisted on a particular core curriculum, with particular lessons to be learned. As a key Fair document reprinted in the book reports, "The plain American citizen will be able to see here what he could attain for his community and himself by intelligent coordinated effort and will be made to realize the interdependence of every contributing form of life and work." Thus the Fair, in the eyes of its planners, proposed not only to invite the people, but to *create* the people in the most ideal sense of the concept.

Making a World's Fair is aware that all fairs have a more general and universal purpose. "They are designed directly to stimulate not only the larger interchange of goods domestically, but an increased international trade. . . . In general, the success they attain in making business in every country aware of its own advantages and disadvantages as compared with others is very great."

In what sense does this perception of the nature of the Fair rest on an idea of the people? There are two significant issues at stake here. This Fair, more than had any previous effort, promoted as a major purpose the availability of consumer goods and services. It was a Fair that from the very start viewed the people not only as observers but as potential consumers of the products it displayed. Indeed, as we shall see, the most popular exhibits tended to be those of producers of consumer goods. Thus, the advertising potential of the Fair and its promotion of the growing consumer culture of the time marked a subtle change in the role of the Fair—for the people. So important was this aspect to the World's Fair Corporation that it established an early Advisory Committee on Consumer Interests to develop some sort of effective consumer program. Yet in February 1939, several months before the Fair was to open, twenty-one members of that committee—government officials, consumer experts, academic and business—resigned, charging that the committee had been used to help sell exhibition space but that there had been "no

The statement reflects dozens of similar ones in speeches, news releases, and brochures issued from 1935, when Fair planning began, through the period of the life of the Fair. Whalen himself reiterated his populist appeal on the very first page of the Fair's *Official Guide Book*: "This is *your* Fair, built for *you*, and dedicated to *you*." In his autobiography, *Mr. New York*, he cited yet another brochure which announced that the Fair was for "everyone" and that its purpose was to "project the average man into the World of Tomorrow." *Making a World's Fair* also reprints an early statement, approved by the board of directors, that referred to their enterprise as "everyman's fair," dedicated to "bearing on the life of the great mass of the people," and offering special insights opportunity to promote the interests of consumers in the planning of exhibits or to afford themselves any safeguard as to the values or reliability of information imparted to them by the Fair." This ambiguous relationship between the Fair and the people-as-consumers was to pervade the following two years.

While *Making a World's Fair* acknowledges that fairs can be successful even if there is a financial loss for the Fair itself, it is equally convinced that a fair's contribution to world business and social progress would be more "limited" if this were the case. Thus from the start the Corporation assumed two additional and urgent functions: the Corporation itself would make money and its bondholding investors would reap a just profit. There was considerable confidence that New York City would also receive enormous financial gains. Whalen insisted that the Fair would bring to New York visitors who would spend a total of a billion dollars for merchandise, entertainment, hotels, and the like. Indeed, he calculated that an average Fair visitor would spend $56 in New York, of which $3.92 would be spent at the Fair itself.

It was in this way that the people, or the average Americans as the Fair executives called them, also meant what *Making a World's Fair* called "gates." The lesson is clear: "a cardinal principle of every fair is to have enough unusual, varied, and preferably

'revolutonary' spectacles and entertainments to attract masses of people, at an entrance fee that will not discourage volume attendance." In addition to their new role as consumers, the people were now customers.

Another aspect of the Fair's perspective on the people is more difficult to document, having received too little discussion in connection with almost all World's Fairs and perhaps especially with this one. In his introduction to *Making . . .*, Whalen writes of the "color and rhythm and music and festivity" of the Fair; in his autobiography, he called the Fair "a rich and colorful festival." We know, of course, of the importance of color at the Fair and the special qualities attained through remarkable lighting. But let us consider the Fair as Festival, complete with parades, bands, pageants, and ceremonial occasions—the daily programs, the state salutes, and the vital participation of Fairgoers (the people) in these ritualistic activities. Whalen himself was a master of pomp and ceremony. He had arranged the extraordinary 1927 New York reception for Lindbergh and staged a brilliant National Recovery Act parade in New York City. Even the newspaper accounts of the many ceremonial events that made up the daily calendar at the Fair are alive with the spirit of popular involvement, with a sense of engagement ritualized.

Grover Whalen with "Grover's Boys," from the cast of a New York theatrical revue. "What, no carnations?" quipped the caption. (PMW)

If the Fair had been a small medieval festival in France or Italy, there undoubtedly would be a scholarly monograph on its meaning and significance. But in the United States we seldom take our festival life seriously. However, Whalen and the board of directors took the festival aspect of the Fair with all due seriousness. Whalen was a master showman, who listed himself in *Who's Who* as a merchant, and his merchandising of the Fair often showed genius.

For the Fair was more than a plan, a well-ordered architectural and artistic display, brilliantly illuminated and effectively colored. It was as well a festival of sight and sound—always sound. The colorful tractor trains that toured the Fairgrounds played a few bars of "The Sidewalks of New York," and there were always bands, orchestras, and even, from some exhibits, the allure of interior sound floating out onto the general grounds. One *New York Times* item on May 5, 1939 speaks for a hundred or more similar reports:

> Bands of strolling players—singers, dancers, musicians, acrobats, clowns, hired by the management Friday—roamed about the Fair. Seen in exhibit and amusement areas, they were strumming banjoes, singing popular songs, giving out swing music. They were always surrounded by crowds wherever they went.

Whalen knew the Fair could never be limited to the dream world of education and enlightenment its planners had envisioned; it had to meet the demands of its tenants, those commercial interests who regarded their participation as a simple money-making proposition. But in promising both enlightenment and consumer delights, Whalen was offering more than any fair could deliver.

The occasion for the Fair was the celebration of the 150th anniversary of the inauguration of George Washington as president, on the steps of Federal Hall in New York. When Fair ticket sales were not up to expectations in August 1939, Whalen organized a "Jubilee Campaign" to sell 600,000 tickets in two weeks. Three hundred Fair employees—police, cashiers, guides, Haskell Indians, information clerks, and actors and actresses from Fair attractions—proceeded from the Fair grounds in a vast motorcade to Wall Street and the very spot at which Washington's inaugural ceremony had been held. There songs and stunts were performed at the base of the Washington statue; the music of the Trytons, the Fair Band, and the Dagenham Pipers (from the entertainment "Merrie England") helped delight the crowd of over 10,000. George McAneny, a banker and chairman of the Fair's board of directors, addressed the crowd, urging them to buy tickets to "your own Fair." It would be he promised:

> an experience and an opportunity to remember throughout your lives. We want you all to come, and we know that most of you will, but because there are still some slackers among so many thousands, some of the Fair employees have come to tell you a bit more about the Fair.

The "World's Fair Champion Hitchhiker" made it to the Fair from Detroit in four days. (NYP)

Bill Robinson of "The Hot Mikado" danced and a group of chorus girls from another attraction did the *Can-Can*. Thus was historic celebration transformed for commercial gain; Fair attendance became equated with patriotic duty. The whole occasion had become a carnival.

One way in which the 1930s defined the people was in terms of Public Opinion. This concept had acquired an official aura after 1935, with the establishment by George Gallup of the American Institute of Public Opinion. Gallup's organization developed a method of polling which enabled all Americans to know what average or typical Americans thought about leading issues of the day. Thus in August 1939 Gallup was able to report that at least 85 percent of those who attended the Fair enjoyed it. Women were found to be significantly more enthusiastic about it than men. The "typical Fair visitor" visited the Fair an average of 2.3 times and only 3 percent of those attending didn't like the Fair at all. Significantly, of those who didn't attend the Fair, 63 percent felt they could not afford to attend.

In May Gallup reported that Fair visitors liked the following exhibits best: General Motors, the Theme Center (Democracity), American Telephone and Telegraph, Ford Motor Company, Soviet Pavilion, British Pavilion, and the Railroad exhibit.

During the same year Gallup reported other popular attitudes that might very well be important in a final assessment of the relationship between the people and the Fair. The majority of

Americans thought the most serious issue facing the nation was not unemployment (the second most important issue) but keeping out of the war. The percentage for this as an overriding issue grew as the year came to an end. Few people seemed interested in buying television sets (13 percent) and there was still considerable doubt (47 percent) among the unemployed about whether one or the other spouse would be able to get a job within the next two years. And perhaps most interesting of all—given the Fair's enthusiasm for The World of Tomorrow and the wonders of machine technology—a June survey of those on relief disclosed that the reason most often given for the cause of their unemployment (23 percent) was the increased use of machines. Here was a paradox that Fair planners had hardly imagined in their optimistic vision of the technological future.

The real genius of the exhibitors at the Fair—and the Fair's Board of Design—was their understanding that the machine itself was not to be central, as it traditionally had been in all world's fairs since 1851 and the Crystal Palace. Rather, they realized that in a consumer-centered society people ended up more fascinated with *process* than with machines. This Fair *showed* its visitors the processes. In this respect the intellectuals who planned the Fair and the people who attended it may have found some measure of interaction.

The people played yet another role. The designers and the theme committee did all they could to dramatize the sights of the Fair but the people of the People's Fair contributed a new element of singular innovation. It is perhaps best described in "Drama and Crowds—Direct Sources of and Materials for Design," an editorial that appeared in the August 1940 issue of *Architectural Record*:

> Yet the greatest discovery in New York was the discovery of the crowd both as actor and as decoration of great power. The designers found out that the crowd's greatest pleasure is in the crowd.

There followed a brilliant review of the most successful exhibits—A.T.&T., Westinghouse, and General Motors—where the crowd took on a decorative pattern or where it was effectively used to fill space to excite the interest of other visitors. "Was not the finest element in the World's Fair 'theme center' the 'helicline,' with that long line of *people* held confidently against the sky?" the reviewer asked. "The people themselves could well be the chief drama and decoration of a public architecture. . . ."

The official photographic version of the Fair experience—compiled in the commercial newsreels and the professionally commissioned photographs of the time—presents only one dimension of a much broader record. From opening day the people turned their Fair into something particularly special and vital to them: a setting for a series of important personal photographic souvenirs. No one can estimate the number of pictures—or the number of full photographic albums—that amateur photographers created out of their Fair. The newspapers were constantly reporting the rescue of amateur photographers who found themselves in dangerous situations while snapping pictures, and the Fair managers devoted more and more time to enabling camera-snapping visitors to accomplish their pictures without interfering with the life of the Fair. A study of the images they collected and how they visualized themselves and their families and friends within the Fair's environment would provide us with an invaluable understanding of the Fair from the people's perspective.

The Fair was not open for long before the people showed both the planners and the commercial interests how perverse they could be about following the arrangements so carefully made for them. One incident stands as a symbol for those who would dare to plan such an exposition in a world of modern capitalism. During the months of June and July 1939, the newspapers reported the dilemma frequently, and experts—planners, psychologists, and other professionals—provided their best official opinions and advice. What had happened was that 75 percent of the visitors who entered the Fairgrounds from subway and railroad terminals were turning to the right as they arrived, refusing absolutely to use both of the ramps provided for them. Fair officials and the newspapers insisted they did this in groups, "like sheep," and the situation not only created serious traffic problems but exasperated those exhibitors whose locations were on the left. In the end, in spite of the battery of official solutions, the people proceeded on its own way.

Nothing is more characteristic of the 1930s vision of the people than the concept of the typical or the average. While several suggestive examples already have been provided, a few more will confirm how central this vision was to the Fair during both its years.

Even before the Fair opened, in February 1939, the Consolidated Edison Company had announced that as a part of its theme it would display the high standard of living achieved by its 37,000 employees. This was to be accomplished by using the figure of Bill Jones, and a display of the living standard he had reached in 1938, as typical of all the Edison employees. A statue of Jones was to dominate the exhibit, which would highlight the facts that he was earning one-sixth more money for a shorter work week than in 1929, that he was a member of the Edison Savings and Loan Association, and that he was a happy participant in the Edison employee life insurance program. Bill was also portrayed as being safer from accidents than non-Edison workers, boasting a health rating more than 30 percent higher than the average industrial worker. Comprehensive medical insurance was his, as was the ability to get a low-interest loan that allowed him to be a homeowner.

In September 1940 the Fair selected New York City's typical boy on the basis of his appearance and his essay on the typical American boy. The winner, suitably enough, was to pose for a statue of the typical American boy. He was Alfred Roberts, Jr., an eighth-grader at P.S. 53, and his prize-winning essay was reprinted in the *New York Times*. It is a document clearly reflective of the values the Fair held dear:

> The typical American boy should possess the same qualities as those of the early American pioneers. He

Crowds entering the Fair via the IRT-BMT subway bridge. (NYP)

should be handy, dependable, courageous, and loyal to his beliefs. He should be clean, cheerful, and friendly, willing to help and be kind to others. He is an all-around boy—interested in sports, hobbies, and the world around him.

The typical American boy takes good care of the public property he uses. He enjoys the comics, the movies, outdoor games, pets, and radio programs. He is usually busy at some handicraft or hobby and is always thinking up something new to do or make. That is why America still has a future.

One of the Fair's most popular films, *I'll Tell the World*, was shown every half-hour at the Macfadden Publications exhibit; it followed the pattern of the family series so successful during the 1930s. Starring Jed Prouty, the Mauch Twins, and other leading performers of the day, it was the saga of how a typical American family, faced with the failure of its father's business, is "restored to happiness and security when father discovers the miraculous powers of advertising." (The quotation is from a *New York Times* report on March 5, 1939.) As expertly developed in the 1920s, the candid aim of advertising was to create a demand for its producers' goods and services. Then, as Silas Bent, the long-time investigator of American foibles in a machine-made nation, summed up in 1932, the four main emotions that advertising played on were humor, health, fear, and sentiment. A number of consumer advocates argued for resistance to such mass psychology. Stuart Chase, for example, maintained that if American society was to be truly functional, advertising would be used to teach people about the actual merits of new products, inventions, and opportunities; there would be no need to rely on psychological conditioning to foster artificial demand. In a *Survey* article on November 1, 1928, Chase referred to Russia as a country in which advertising was functional as well as beautiful.

The Fair took these arguments seriously, becoming in itself a gigantic advertisement both for a functional society and for the ideals and values that might produce such a society. Abandoning the old mass psychology appeals the major exhibitors followed suit. In 1933 General Motors issued a pamphlet, "The Philosophy of Customer Research," detailing its newer version of its relationship with the public—the potential consumers of its products. A summary statement from the work, which was issued almost annually during the 1930s, reveals its perspective:

> If a company can ascertain concretely and in detail just what the buyers would like to have, if it can build products in conformity with those desires and design its sales and advertising messages so that they will answer definitely the questions that are uppermost in the mind of the motorist, obviously there will be continued improvement in the merchandising process and a broadening of the service rendered.

Many of the most popular exhibits at the Fair attempted to follow this proposal by demonstrating *process* to involve the potential customer, by answering his or her questions, and by making the visitor feel part of the operation in a dramatic way. This is not to say that there were no hard-sell efforts to mold opinion and to stimulate interest in particular styles and approaches, but the fact of the visitor's involvement and participation shows that a new mode of advertising was pioneered in a major way at the Fair. This was indeed a new relationship between the people and the producers.

However, there were contradictions in the Fair's ideology concerning the people. Among them is the melancholy fact that the planners proposed, from the start, three important centers that were clearly off limits to the people. There were three private clubs at the Fair: Perylon Hall, the center of official entertaining, the Club of the National Advisory Committee, and the Terrace Club, of even more limited membership, restricted to certain major Fair bondholders.

Although the Fair planners saw to it that their experiences and ideology were preserved for posterity, we have fewer documents easily available to assess how the people in turn perceived the Fair. We can interpret only indirectly the impressions of those who attended, or who only read about it, saw pictures or movies of it, or received accounts from those who did attend.

The enterprise itself was an economic failure. The Chicago Fair in 1933 had made money; New York was convinced it could do even better. It didn't. Attendance never matched expectations. Polls and press agents predicted that fifty million would attend during the first of the Fair's two seasons but even two years of the Fair did not reach that mark. Why? A general explanation that seems to have satisfied most interpreters is the cost: the 75¢ admission charge was excessive.

Harvey Dow Gibson, a banker who served on the executive committee of the Fair board and who ran the Fair in

Harvey Gibson, Chairman of the Board of Directors of the Fair Corporation. (PMW)

1940, insisted that a 50¢ admission, universal at all other fairs at the time, would have made the enterprise successful by drawing more people. Other critics agreed with Gardner Harding, in his generally approving *Harper's* analysis, that the "price ranges of the Fair are not . . . geared to the pocketbook of the fifty million people whom the Fair has staked its credit (and its return to its bondholders) on attracting through its turnstiles." He figured that an average tour of the Fair's high spots, with reasonable meals for two people, would cost an alarming $7.00.

Yet Gibson's privately printed autobiography, written in 1951, suggests another possibility (and incidentally offers an explanation for some of the changes that took place during the 1940 season, when he was in charge):

> The Fair opened with overpowering ceremony, great pomp, and with regal splendor. So much so, that the common run of people, especially those from small places throughout the country, which were counted upon to comprise the backbone of the attendance, seemed to become sort of frightened in a way by it all and were ill at ease rubbing elbows or at the prospect of doing so, with what had unfortunately become known throughout the country as the high silk hat group which seemed to them as predominating.

There seemed to be a growing feeling on the part of the masses expected to rush for the gates that they would be out of place in such an atmosphere.

But what of those who did come? The first conclusion that seems obvious from the published sources is that there was little interest in either the theme or the Fair's meticulous plan. The carefully articulated zones, the focal exhibits, the imaginative and symbolic use of color—they seemed to make no impression that in any way shaped consciousness in terms of what the Fair planners had seen as their message. Joseph Wood Krutch in the *Nation* carefully recommended that Fair visitors avoid "buildings given large inclusive titles like 'Food,' 'Communications,' 'Consumers,' and the like." He stressed the Fair as a public playground and made fun of the whole effort to define the World of Tomorrow. Debunking the educational and cultural exhibits, he delighted in the "showmanship . . . so good . . . that science and industry provide spectacles which could easily compete with acrobats and trained seals of a conventional circus."

Life gave the Fair a major picture essay ("Life Goes to the World's Fair," July 3, 1939) and detailed its favorite moments and exhibitions but remained remarkably uninterested in the social message. Instead it saw "a magnificent monument by and to American business." Walter Lippmann, in his influential column, did comment on the magnificent technological achievement of America, but he found it ironic in view of men's lack of "moral unity with their fellows and moral equilibrium within themselves."

Again and again, the critics admired and enjoyed the Fair's entertainment but seemed unimpressed with its theme and higher purpose. Krutch, in the *Nation*, was bored with the message of Democracity; he complained about its 25¢ admission charge and fussed at some technical difficulties experienced during his visit. But he was captivated by the spectacle of Bel Geddes's Crystal Lassies: "One stands on a platform just outside a huge crystal polygon while nude dancers, deliriously multiplied by reflection, dance on the mirror floors." So much for the Fair's message.

Gardner Harding, the Fair's friendliest critic, aired the most fundamental objection to its practices by quoting an apologia from a Fair administrator who had been with the project from the beginning:

> . . . to be fully representative of community interests, the Fair should have included the cooperative movement, the granges and farmers' groups, the many useful and important social organizations that make up life in every American community. But you can't sell space to those folks. They haven't any money.

Harding's own comment was that these folks without money were "anticipating the World of Tomorrow with the rest of us" and that they were hardly a minority of Americans. As an example of this failure he provided a lengthy analysis of the Fair-sponsored Town of Tomorrow, which he described as a "breach of faith." The exhibit intended to demonstrate that an actual modern residential community could be built with the materials of the present for the pocketbook of everyman. After reminding his readers that three-quarters of Americans earned less than three thousand dollars a year, Harding pointed out that, of the sixteen houses in the exhibit, only six "meet the absolute minimum requirement of social usefulness in costing less than $10,000 apiece."

The media that covered the Fair with perhaps the most intense interest and concern were the business magazines. For them the story of the Fair was a question of sheer marketing: advertising, merchandising, selling. *Business Week* did a long analysis on November 4, 1939, attempting to account for the success of the "shows that pulled at the Fair." General Motors's Futurama (*Business Week* felt people liked the comfortable moving chairs) was clearly the hit attraction. Others included: Eastman Kodak, with its brilliant show of photographs; American Telephone and Telegraph's audience participation, with free long-distance calls and the VODER, a device that talked like a human (*Business Week* felt the pretty girl operator who worked the keys and pedals was the secret of its success); and General Electric's House of Magic ("not many in the packed audiences understood the significance of the tricks they saw performed with thyratrons and stroboscopes. But they came away thrilled, mystified, and soundly sold on the company"). G.E. also featured a kitchen in which the appliances talked.

Reflecting the success of the general philosophy expressed in the General Motors pamphlet, *Business Week* observed: "Companies making consumer products did a better job of contacting the public than did the industrial goods producers." It admired the Ford exhibit for the comfort of its facilities and the quality of its attendants, who could explain technical matters in a layman's language. Macfadden Publications rated special praise for its clever use of films, "an ideal vehicle for the exhibitor who has something intangible to sell."

The magazine also approved of those solid exhibits that showed manufacturing operations, "sure-fire attractions" at Firestone, Ford, Chrysler, White Owl, and Swift. Exhibitors were critical of the architecture at the Fair, for merchandising reasons, it was reported. Exteriors, several felt, ought to be redesigned to "offer a stronger invitation to come on in."

Although the perspective is special, the list of the most popular exhibits is typical: account after account stresses showmanship above all other values. It is hard to believe that the people didn't respond overwhelmingly.

One major violation of the Fair's ideology turned out to be a remarkable success story in terms of significant profit on investment: Billy Rose's Aquacade, which rated the distinction of a *Time* cover story. The saga of Rose's triumph—approximately one out of every six visitors to the Fair paid 40¢ admission to see his show—is a show business legend. In spite of the fact that many of the Fair managers thought his kind of production totally inappropriate for their lofty vision of the World of Tomorrow, Rose had snagged the choicest ready-built concession for 10 percent under the highest bidders.

Walter Lippmann noticed the irony of G.M.'s extraordinary success with Futurama. "General Motors has spent a small fortune to convince the American public that if it wishes to enjoy the full benefit of private enterprise in motor manufacturing," he wrote, "it will have to rebuild its cities and its highways by public enterprise." Did the people, from their comfortable seats at a fascinating show, notice the contradiction?

Many of the more than 200 films shown at the Fair presented viewers with a complex new relationship between entertainment, education, and deceptively hard-sell commercial messages. The *New York Times* reported on June 18, 1939 that "only a handful" could be classified as pure entertainment. In Whalen's World of Tomorrow, the screen had been converted into a fast-talking salesman.

The *Times* analyzed at length the promotion and content of one of this new breed, *The Middleton Family at the New York World's Fair*. Produced by Westinghouse, it purported to be the story of a middle-class family from Indiana and their adventures at the Fair. In an elaborate advertising and distribution scheme, Westinghouse furnished prints to its local dealers throughout the country, ostensibly so that the people back home would not be deprived of experiencing the Fair's delights. But the Middletons were a fictitious family, portrayed by professional actors, and the Westinghouse Fair Building was the only one the film identified by name. The Fair had become a locus for pioneering what the *Times*, in its headline, dubbed "Tomorrow's Propaganda."

Other events raised questions of whether the American people were, in fact, ready for the World of Tomorrow. The Fair itself and its planners and administrators projected an optimism and an enthusiasm that often bewildered and even angered visitors from Europe, who were witnesses to the coming of a world war. But was this optimism characteristic? Were Americans truly committed to this vision of their future? One of the deans of

The D. E. Leathers family of Clarendon, Texas, selected by a committee of New York newspapermen as one of the "Typical American Families," receives the keys to a new Ford Super Deluxe Fordor sedan, courtesy of the Ford Motor Company. (NYP)

American photography, Edward Steichen, thought not. Speaking at a meeting held to award prizes in a photography contest sponsored by the Citizen's Housing Council, Steichen took the occasion to attack the gloomy subject matter of American art. In the contest for photographs on How New York Lives, 702 photos were submitted, of which 678 portrayed slum scenes, and twenty-four pictured new-model housing. Steichen felt called upon to comment on this in contrast to what he had seen in the photo-murals at the Soviet Pavilion at the Fair. The photography itself, he remarked, was the kind any big American commercial house would regard as the lowest type of work. "But you leave that room after seeing those photographs with a sense of exhilaration. The pictures have joy, gaiety, and life. There's the message. They believe in what they are doing." Steichen seemed to forget the enthusiastic promise of the future that pervaded such art as *The City*, the classic 1930s film that premiered at the Fair. But which of these attitudes was closer to the truth of the people?

What is the historian to make of the fact that the lively and sustained discussion of the Fair's plan and theme, which occupied newspapers and popular magazines for three years before it opened, seemed to disappear once the Fair was a reality? Did the people refuse to accept its ideology, just as they insisted on going their own way, "like sheep?"

The contradictions of the Fair were the contradictions of the culture itself. How well anyone understood the people—except perhaps the newly developing geniuses of advertising and marketing—remains a serious question.

It is interesting to examine some of the significant changes that were made when the Fair reopened in 1940 with Harvey Dow Gibson, the banker, in effect replacing Grover Whalen. Whalen stayed on as figurehead at a cut in pay from $100,000 to $75,000; Gibson worked for nothing in an effort to save the Corporation from bankruptcy. He didn't succeed, but he did manage a profit for the year.

The tone was changed. Gibson announced that the Fair would now be a "super country fair," and the description seems to have been an accurate one. He did away with any talk about the lessons of interdependence; even the World of Tomorrow tended to disappear under the new banner, "For Peace and Freedom," Internationalism was played down, and the emphasis was distinctly American. The Fair's 1940 poster featured a rosy-cheeked, middle-aged, middle-American signifying his great pleasure in same with a caption that read "Makes you proud of your country." A decade or so earlier, people might have called the posterman Babbitt, but the Fair chose to name him Elmer. Actors portraying him made personal appearances all over the country to urge fellow Americans to come to the Fair.

The Soviet Pavilion had been torn down. In its place, newly landscaped, a bandstand was built, and the area was rechristened the American Common. Here various Americanized foreign groups and other American folk performers presented weekly programs of song and dance. Robert Kohn, who from the beginning had been associated with the theme committee and with the board of design and had been the most outspoken proponent of the Fair's

original ideology, was now reduced to presiding over the entertainment there. It is not without significance that an interest in *folk*—perhaps another way of defining the people—replaced the social ideas that had dominated the planning before 1939.

Except for the physical plan itself and its basic iconography—now almost quaint because it failed to function as part of a fundamental unity of thought and action—it was difficult to detect much that had survived from the first Fair season to the second. The Consumers Building was now the World of Fashion, complete with fashion shows. There were two new model houses, erected according to FHA standards, on the grounds before the Electrified Farm. These became homes for "more than forty representative American families, who will stay one week each. The families will be selected by newspapers in various parts of the country, and will consist of a father American, a mother American, and two little Americans, preferably a boy and a girl." One thing the Fair was not about to forget was its dedication to the average American and the average American family.

General Motors's 1940 additions included trains and still more cars on the roads of its exhibit. Bel Geddes, yielding to those who had found serious lapses in his vision of 1960, added 600 more churches, several hundred filling stations, and one university.

The 1940 emphasis on a folksy, comfortable Fair clearly suggested an event intended to entertain and amuse as opposed to one which challenged the mind. The Gibson administration renamed the Fair's entertainment area The Great White Way, and the Fair managers were more helpful to concessioners than they had been under Whalen's tenure.

The 1940 *Official Guide Book* was completely revised in a style designed to be snappier and more popular than the 1939 version. Stanley Applebaum, in the excellent introductory essay to his *The New York World's Fair 1939/40*, a selection of professional photographs, compares a 1939 guide book entry with its 1940 successor: 1939's "In Steimetz Hall, vivid lightning, thunderous noise, ten million volts flashing over a thirty-foot arc" became 1940's "In Steinmetz Hall, 10,000,000 volts of man-made lightning leap thirty feet through the air with a roar of thunder, scaring the daylights out of you."

The coming of war to Europe—and the well-documented fear of Americans that they somehow might be drawn into it—obviously cast a shadow on the Fair during both years of its existence. Wyndam Lewis, who came to visit the Fair from an England in the midst of struggle with Nazi Germany, provided a chilling comparison in his *America, I Presume* (1940). Unable to believe that the Fair could be as innocent as it seemed, he likened the Court of Power to the spectacle of the Nuremberg Rally.

The managers decided early on not to broadcast news of the war at the Fairgrounds, but this could hardly obliterate the increasing consciousness of Americans about what the war meant. The theme committee had struggled to instill an understanding of interdependence that would assure peace; now the 1940 Fair was acknowledging the coming of war, sponsoring, for example, special occasions for peoples and governments in exile.

A final assessment of The People's Fair is difficult, for the people remain an anomaly. They were shown the possibilities of life as a festival, as a magic show, and they accepted consumer capitalism without critical reflection because of the wonders of process unfolded before them. So it was that the Fair became a rather generalized advertisement for something the 1930s had begun to call the American Way of Life.

The Fair's influence on the directions of science, technology, and the arts is a visible one. In an article about "Trends of Tomorrow," *House and Garden* predicted that the new ideas in home decoration displayed there "will surely bend the collective American mind to a much more widespread acceptance of the modern idiom—in architecture, decoration, and landscaping." The magazine's prediction was accurate, but the sectors it chose to feature—the Fair's three private clubs, the executive suites of the major exhibitors, the foreign pavilions of Poland, Finland, and Sweden—were either off limits to the people or sparsely attended in favor of the more spectacular attractions. It was the Fair *itself* that became a useful advertisement, in quite the same way that Thorstein Veblen had suggested in 1899: high culture becomes a kind of advertisement for the leisure class and those who would emulate it. For the people, the World of Tomorrow projected not a new world, but a new fantasy world based on the possibilities of modern technology, a world that could be enjoyed because it could be controlled—a veritable Disneyland.

Although physically vanished, the Trylon and the Perisphere remain as indelible as icons for all Americans. Although few can remember their specific symbolic import and what lesson they proposed to teach, all the people held on to the image; it is part of our legacy from the 1930s, a dazzling white reminder of a world that somehow science and technology might achieve, a neat and ordered geometric pattern which pleased aesthetically but somehow, like a science fiction movie set, seemed alien to life as it is really lived.

If few remember what that image signified, fewer still are aware of what actually became of it. The four thousand tons of steel that went into the making of the Trylon and Perisphere became scrap destined to make bombs and other instruments of war. Designed to teach lessons of mutual interdependence which would make all future wars impossible, in its own final functioning the symbol became an instrument of war.

Given the contradictions between the planners' ideology and the demands of consumer capitalism, perhaps we can only guess what the New York World's Fair of 1939/1940 means as history. Perhaps, as John Bainbridge and St. Clair McKelvey observed in the *New Yorker* ("That Was the New York World's Fair") after it closed, the most eloquent summation of the whole Flushing incident "was made by a radio man named Dave Driscoll, an expert in double-talk" who worked for New York's station WOR:

> On closing night, after everyone else said farewell to the Fair, Driscoll mounted the dais in the Court of Peace wearing top hat and tails and spoke impromptu in a tongue unknown to Barnum, as follows: 'In this

Cast members of the "American Jubilee" invite Fair visitors of 1940 to the Great White Way, the renamed and revamped Amusement zone. (NYP)

vast amphitheatre millions from all the Americas and from all corners of the world have heard addresses by statesmen, Whalen, graisnas, McAneny, cabishon, Gibson, forbine, and nobility. Here was the pledge of peace which might well have been the fiederness, bedistran, and goodle of this great expedition. Now that pledge is forgotten. Sleedment, twaint, and broint forbish the doldrum all over the world. Alas!'

We might all learn to double-talk. Or perhaps we might better learn to face and resolve the contradictions.

Warren I. Susman, Professor of History at Rutgers University, is an American cultural historian. He is the author of *Culture and Commitment, 1929-1945*.

THE DESIGN OF REASON: Architecture and Planning at the 1939/40 New York World's Fair

Eugene A. Santomasso

The Fair is a dramatic and manifold demonstration of the arts and their uses in creating order, design and harmony in the environment evolved by modern society.

Holger Cahill in *American Art Today New York World's Fair*, 1939

A VISION OF THE FUTURE

In October 1936 the New York World's Fair Corporation and its president, Grover Whalen, officially declared the theme of the 1939/1940 World's Fair to be "Building the World of Tomorrow," and announced their intention to "immediately start building the greatest international exposition in history."[1] The decade had been marked by a wave of fairs in Europe and in America. It had been ushered in by the 1930 Stockholm Fair which was followed by the 1933 Chicago "Century of Progress" Exposition; then, in quick succession there were fairs in Paris, 1937, Glasgow 1938, and, in 1939, it was closed by fairs held simultaneously in New York and San Francisco.

New York City had already hosted the first American fair in 1853, the "Crystal Palace" which had celebrated America as a center of unity and brotherhood. The Fair was to be the culmination of this nineteenth-century tradition, in which expositions were promoted to stimulate local business and to glorify the community in the name of a national celebration. The event to be celebrated in 1939 was the 150th anniversary of George Washington's inauguration. At the end of a decade of depression, and in the face of world tyranny and holocaust, New York City was to host the Fair of fairs.

The Theme and Other Fairs

Earlier fairs, and especially American fairs, had focused on the relation between art and technology.[2] The Philadelphia Centennial Exposition of 1876 had treated the arts and the potentials of technological innovation as separate entities, while the 1893 Columbian Exposition in Chicago had promoted a new relation between them, predicting an American cultural Renaissance of unsurpassed beauty, harmony, and permanence. And the 1933 Chicago Fair had introduced Americans to a yet different synthesis of art and technology. In this conception, science, industry, business, education, and mass entertainment were drawn together in an effort to convey the vital pulse and energy of twentieth-century society. The Fair was to extend the Chicago developments and to impart an entirely new perspective.

As at Chicago, the Fair sought to appeal to the mass public, and in this endeavor the architecture and displays were to make extensive use of scientific and technological advances as well as various techniques of corporate communication and advertising. While the 1933 Fair had shown the future as science fiction, the New York planners conceived of it as an attainable goal, presented on a grand scale in the tangible from of elements from commerce and industry, expanded via architecture and art. Design and daily life were conceived of as being one. The Fair visitor was to be thrust into the full-blown Age of Consumerism and the Age of the Machine. The most prominent features of these were streamlined form, fluorescent lighting, the automobile, and the roadway. It was their potential, the planners believed, that would transform and elevate American daily life.

World's Fairs traditionally are considered to be places of experimentation, where structures for the most part are impermanent, where the festive spirit excuses the inventions of form and structure from the necessity for utilitarian logic. The Fair did not abound in radical or overt feats of structural engineering, and in this sense it differed from both Chicago 1933 and Paris 1937. Instead, the qualities of invention present at the Fair were outgrowths of its futuristic theme and of its special melding of design, commercial objectives, and industrial technology. Unlike Stockholm 1930, the architecture of the Fair did not feature the pure principles of modern design known as the International Style; unlike Paris 1937, the architecture was more than a series of engineering spectacles, or the sophisticated refinement of modernistic devices and ideas that flourished at the end of the decade; and unlike San Francisco 1939, the architecture was not a fantastic stage set that evoked a lost paradise. Indeed, the disparate character of the Fair's architecture confounded most of its critics. It embodied elements of the International Style, the popular moderne concepts, and the academic Beaux-Arts school, combining them with the most advanced ideas from advertising and industrial design.[3] To grasp the Fair's architecture as a whole is to appreciate the pluralism of its form, vocabulary, symbolic meaning, and the varied quality of its design.

The Background to Architectural Planning for the Fair

The essential policies for the Fair's architecture and planning were established between May and October 1936, largely the outgrowth of and a response to a controversy raging in New York artistic circles over what should constitute the appropriate character of the forthcoming Fair. Spearheading the controversy was "The Fair of the Future Committee," guided by the critic and historian Lewis Mumford. Adopting a progressive point of view, the committee feared that the Fair's architecture could easily degenerate into a pastiche of the Neoclassicism that was then current in architectural design and favored by the conservatively oriented American Institute of Architects. The committee shuddered at the possibility of a "Parthenon on a Flushing Swamp."[4] They proposed that the Fair's relevance would be ensured by the tenets of modern architecture, coupled with an appropriate social theme.

The Fair of the Future Committee recommended that an architectural board be charged with the responsibility for coordinating the Fair's general plan and architectural design. As a result, a seven-member design board was formed in May 1936; in September, in keeping with the committee's belief that open competition was the most effective means of turning up fresh talent, it launched an architectural competition.[5]

Broad powers were given to the design board.[6] It was to be responsible for directing the theme of the Fair, and for determining its plan, construction types and standards, and general architectural characteristics, including color and lighting. The board was empowered to recommend all architects, designers, and engineers, and to exercise final approval over all construction. For the most part, the membership of the board represented the conservative

wing in architectural politics: its chairman, Stephen F. Voorhees, was the current president of the American Institute of Architects; two other members were past presidents of the A.I.A.; and another currently served on the A.I.A. board of directors. One design board member outside this group was the industrial designer, Walter Dorwin Teague. A participant in the controversy sparked by the Fair of the Future Committee, Teague was a voice of moderation, suggesting that earlier fairs be studied for their functional aspects and warning architects to restrain themselves from turning the Fair into an "aesthetic orgy."[7] Due largely to his influence, New York 1939 was to become an industrial designer's Fair, bringing Teague together with Norman Bel Geddes, Henry Dreyfuss, Donald Deskey, and Raymond Loewy.

One of the design board's main concerns was the effective wedding of architectural values with those of commerce and industry. The board's decision to sponsor an architectural competition was a reversal of its original position against holding such a contest. It first had been proposed that the Board solicit certain architects to submit designs for specific buildings at the Fair. The sentiment favoring open competition initially expressed by the Committee was bolstered by the A.I.A.'s official policy of supporting architectural competitions for public buildings. Fair officials had high expectations of the competitive design for a "typical fair building," not only because it might uncover new architectural talent, but also, in the words of Grover Whalen, that it might foster designs signaling "the starting point of a new era in building."[8] The contest, limited to registered architects with offices or residences in the New York metropolitan area, brought an overwhelming response; by its closing date, 356 entries had been submitted to the design board. The winning projects demonstrated the board's intentions: the Fair's architecture would embrace Beaux-Arts principles and moderne qualities, billboard art, and industrial styling.[9] A variegated vision was taking shape.

UP FROM THE ASHES AT FLUSHING MEADOW

The first announcements stated that the marshlands and dumping grounds of Flushing would be transformed into a park for the site. The creation of a park in northern Queens to rival the size of Manhattan's Central Park long had been the cherished dream of City Parks Commissioner Robert Moses. The Fair was to be the means to realize it. A complex reclamation scheme, set into motion with state and federal funds secured by Moses, recast the meandering wasteland of Flushing Creek into an ordered landscape of lakes, canals, and plantings.[10] The site of the Fair was a 3¼ mile tract of land, roughly wedge-shaped, stretching northward toward its widest point, adjacent to Flushing Bay. Compared with Manhattan, the land parcel may be loosely conceived as extending in width from Tudor City to Times Square, in length from Central Park South to Broome Street.

The large central portion of the site was reserved for the main exhibit area; the narrower southern end, developed around a man-made lake, became the Amusement zone. A total of 1,216 acres made the Fair site second in area only to the Louisiana Purchase Exposition of 1904.

The Site

The rail and rapid transit lines and the metropolitan parkway system that served the site were determinative factors in the planning. Traversing the site, splitting it into unequal segments, was the Grand Central Parkway, which had been completed in 1932 and which, with W.P.A. funding, was widened for the Fair. Clustered at the northern periphery of the site were the elevated tracks of the IRT and BMT transit systems, the tracks of the Long Island Railroad, and parking lots for cars and buses. A new LIRR station, a temporary structure, extended two ramps from the concourse level to one of the Fair's plazas. To the south, at the juncture of the main and amusement areas, the IND subway station was located—another temporary structure which was erected in conjunction with a special project that extended the IND transit line to the Fairground. West of the IND station was a second parking lot, across from the Amusement zone on the other side of Grand Central Parkway.

The locations of the various transportation systems required multiple entrances to the grounds. Placed at the periphery of the Fair site, the entrances aligned with the rail and rapid transit points, parking facilities, and bridges that crossed Grand Central Parkway and World's Fair Boulevard—the east-west arterial separating the amusement and main exhibit areas. Two permanent bridges crossing Grand Central Parkway were widened with temporary boardwalks to facilitate the flow of pedestrian traffic between the central portion of the main exhibit area and the large transportation exhibit area across the parkway to the west. The goal was to insure the most efficient movement of the enormous crowds the planners expected.[11]

The Plan

A geometric plan of Beaux-Arts derivation organized the main exhibit area into a *rond-point* system of radiating streets and fanlike segments.[12] Symmetrical axes led to the Fair's central theme building, the Trylon and Perisphere. The longitudinal central axis of Constitutional Mall extended from the Trylon and Perisphere eastward to the oval Lagoon of Nations and beyond, to the Court of Peace, which was flanked by foreign-sponsored pavilions and terminated by the symmetrical U.S. Government Building. Extending at 45° angles from either side of the Trylon and Perisphere were the Avenue of Patriots and the Avenue of Pioneers, both of which culminated in circular plazas—the former at Bowling Green, before the IRT and BMT entrances, and the latter at Lincoln Square. These outlying plazas were linked by an arcing thoroughfare, appropriately named Rainbow Avenue, which bisected the axis of the central mall.

At the Trylon and Perisphere a transverse north-south axis connected the Court of Communications, with its towering pylons, to the Plaza of Light, with its surrounding utilities buildings. The

Mayor La Guardia at Marshall Field in Chicago, on a tour promoting the Fair, October 1938. (FC)

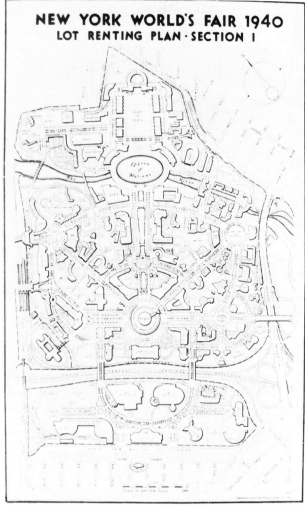

NEW YORK WORLD'S FAIR 1940
LOT RENTING PLAN · SECTION I

Cat. no. 5. (AL)

transverse axis extended southward across World's Fair Boulevard by means of the Empire State Bridge and culminated in the New York State Exhibition Building and the permanent Amphitheater at the near end of Fountain Lake in the amusement zone. Behind the Trylon and Perisphere, to the west, was the permanent New York City Building (now housing The Queens Museum), and beyond it, across the Grand Central Parkway extension, was located the Transportation zone—reached by a pair of overpasses, the Bridge of Wheels and the Bridge of Wings. Peripheral areas of the site were developed into curved roads which connected with the main intersecting axes.

Officials justified the Fair's formal layout on two accounts: that it reinforced the thematic divisions, or sectors, around which the Fair was organized; and that it best facilitated the distribution and circulation of people.[13] Both explanations reflected a Neoclassic attitude associating geometry with clarity and logic of design. An alternative, equally logical, way to organize the Fair was proposed by the architect Ian Woodner-Silverman, a member of The Fair of the Future committee. His plan, an informal serpentine, only brief descriptions of which survive today, was conceived in conjunction with the Committee's innovative proposal and depicted the Fair as an organized flow of the thematic sectors.[14] The Fair's plan, and the serpentine counterproposal, illustrate the point that logic of intention cannot be thought of as inherent in one mode of design. In this regard, it is interesting to note that while the Fair adopted a formal plan believing it would best facilitate the free movement of people, the Chicago fair had adopted an informal plan for exactly the same reason. The major rationale behind the Fair plan, with its axially coodinated avenues and plazas and wedge-shaped plots, was that it dramatized the act of transforming a swampy rubbish dump into a place of ceremonial order *for the design board.*

Contemporary criticism of the Fair's plan was somewhat predictable. Most critics stressed those factors which undermined the plan's Beaux-Arts coherence and unity. The discrepancy between the discrete boundaries originally conceived for the Fair's zones, and the irregular configurations which resulted, was woefully apparent to those who had followed the various stages of the plan's development. The major complaint was that the plan's absolute order was at odds with free patterns of growth and change. It was also pointed out that a major feature of Beaux-Arts planning, the hierarchical build-up of elements around a center, had been seriously weakened at the Fair by the absence of a single main entrance, in preference to the multiple entrances on the site's periphery.

Other features of Beaux-Arts planning were found to be lacking: little had been done to coordinate the scale of elements or to define spatial sequences through changes of level. In this regard, it was pointed out that the vista along Constitution Mall, toward the Trylon and Perisphere, was fragmented by a number of elements, the most obvious of which was the overscaled statue of George Washington. While the Trylon and Perisphere could be seen from virtually every point on the Fairgrounds, an unobstructed view of them was rare—a condition attributed to their faulty location on insufficiently elevated terrain. The critics also found problems of scale and siting in each of the zones, where, they charged, the plan had neglected to provide for continuity between some of the focal buildings and their surroundings.

Among the most severe points of criticism was the alleged failure of the planners to provide prominent sites for the foreign pavilions, a departure from the practice of previous international exhibitions.[15] By relegating foreign governments to the somewhat remote sites around the Lagoon of Nations and the Court of Peace, the planners of the Fair had indeed turned away from world's fair tradition. The decision seems to have been part of the effort to establish the image of a new order at the Fair, with the potentials of American society at its center. For all of the plan's inadequacies and inconsistencies, it did succeed in conveying a dramatic image of this projected new order, with the Trylon and Perisphere as its central symbol.

THE THEME CENTER: SYMBOL OF THE FAIR

When the Fair's theme, "Building the World of Tomorrow," was first announced in October 1936, it was joined to the concept of a Theme Center planned to dominate the site. The design for the center consisted of a pair of 250–foot high towers and a vast semicircular hall for dioramas. As depicted in an early model of the Fair, the twin towers first were conceived to be focal elements to complement the blocky mass of the axially aligned U.S. Government Building. Shortly after the projected theme center was shown, the design board commissioned the architectural firm of Harrison and Fouilhoux to create a new design for it. Its dual purpose was a "trade mark or symbol" for the Fair, and, like the earlier twin-tower scheme, to house a display to conceptualize the World of Tomorrow theme. Harrison and Fouilhoux's design for the Trylon and Perisphere was presented in March 1937. The proposed structures would provide the symbolic element around which the Fair was to be built.[16]

Trylon, Perisphere, and Helicline

Three discrete shapes comprised the new Theme Center: the triangular Trylon-tower, 610–feet high; the globular Perisphere, 180–feet in diameter; and the spiral Helicline, a ramp 950–feet in length. The Trylon and Perisphere were linked by a 65–foot high bridge and encircled by the 18–foot wide Helicline. Visitors entered the Perisphere by means of two escalators contained within the bridge, and exited across the bridge, which interpenetrated the Trylon, and was linked with the Helicline which swept them back to surface level. Within the vast Perisphere, twice the size of Rockefeller Center's Radio City Music Hall, was the elaborately coordinated vision of Henry Dreyfuss's Democracity. Visitors were transported from present reality into a cosmic sphere of future possibilities and then cast onto a circular return. Form and motion were synthesized into a sequence of diagonal entry, rotational enclosure, horizontal egress, and spiraling decline.

The Theme Center was a steel framework supported by a foundation ring of reinforced concrete. The Trylon rose directly from the concrete base; the Perisphere was raised seventeen feet from ground level by eight steel columns. Similar tubular steel columns supported the Helicline. Both Trylon and Perisphere were surfaced with gypsum board painted white; the underside of the Helicline was sheathed in stainless steel. The impression was not of structure—visitors were presented with a fantasy of shimmering surfaces and seeming weightlessness. This effect was enhanced by the Perisphere's circle of eight columns being set within a ring of upward gushing fountains making the sphere appear to float on jets of water.

The Harrison and Fouilhoux office turned out over a thousand sketches and numerous model studies before it produced the final design for the Theme Center. Some of the preliminary ideas were published both in contemporary art and architectural

The Theme Center being prepared for exterior surfacing, late 1938. (PMW)

journals and in the June 1937 issue of the *New York World's Fair Bulletin*. The sphere, the triangle, and the spiral were the archetypal forms predominant in these early studies and the final design of the Theme Center would be a synthesis of these shapes.

The Historical Context

The history of architecture offers a number of interesting design precedents for the Theme Center. Projects by some of the visionary French architects of the late eighteenth century were based upon the compositional and symbolic clarity of pure geometric shapes. As a consequence, many of their designs involved towers, spirals, and spherical buildings. Comparable imagery prevailed in some of the spectacularly engineered projects that were postulated for the Columbian Exposition of 1893. Another echo was the 700-foot high Globe Tower projected in 1906 for Coney Island's Steeplechase Park. Other interpretations of geometric form that relate to the Theme Center are the spheres, towers, and spirals that appear in certain projects of the 1920s by the German Expressionist and Russian Constructivist architects.

Among the most diverse assemblages of visionary designs in the early twentieth century were those created in response to the 1929 International Christopher Columbus Lighthouse Competition. A lighthouse design, by a team of Russian architects (G.T. Krautikoff, J.N. Warentzoff, and A.W. Bounnie), consisted of a beacon tower beside a spherical structure, which is tantalizing for its closeness both to some of the preliminary studies and to the final design for the Theme Center. These nineteenth and early twentieth-century visionary schemes remained unbuilt. In fact, after the famous Paris Celestial Globe of 1900, it was not until 1928 that a spherical structure was executed for the first time, in a five-story office building erected at the Dresden "Technological City" Exposition of that year.[17] Modestly-sized and uninspired in design, the building nevertheless must be ranked as an important antecedent to the Theme Center.

Christopher Columbus Memorial Lighthouse Competition entry, 1929 (Krautikoff, Warentzoff & Bounnie, architects). (EAS)

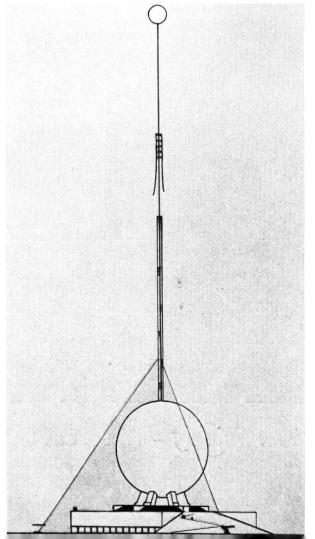

Form and Meaning

The universal appeal of the Theme Center may be attributed to the abstract purity of its forms. Both the Trylon and the Perisphere were immediately recognizable as the symbol of the Fair; in this sense, the Theme Center recalled the Eiffel Tower of the 1889 Paris Fair. Unlike that famous symbol, however, the Theme Center did not reveal its skeleton; instead, it loomed over its surroundings, a remote and scaleless object of alluring clarity and simplicity. The Theme Center's striking modernity was not a result of new forms. It was effective because unadorned basic shapes are associated with stripping away the superfluous in order to get at the essence—a synonym for the modern age of the machine. Grover Whalen expressed this notion in his statement made at the first showing of the design for the Theme Center:

> We promised the world something new in Fair architecture and here it is—something radically different and fundamentally as old as a man's experience . . . . These buildings are themselves a glimpse into the future, a sort of foretaste of that better world of tomorrow, of which we hope in some part to be the harbingers. We feel that simplicity must be the keynote of a perfectly ordered mechanical civilization.

Trylon and Perisphere were timeless images of the concept of a perfect order, and, in the context of the Fair, they symbolized the global aspirations of democracy and of commercial and industrial enterprise.

ARCHITECTURAL IMAGERY AND SYMBOLISM

It was the intention of the design board that the American buildings at the Fair (as distinguished from the foreign pavilions) should embody both a "variety of expressions" and "a measure of unity."[18] Within a controlled setting, the aim was apparently to achieve a festive and stylistically diverse architecture able to captivate the imagination of the visitor without resorting to excessive mannerisms. No doubt the design board wanted to avoid the bizarre modernism and "medley of chizzle chuzzle forms" that critics had found to be so disconcerting at the Chicago fair. Any critical appraisal of the Fair's architecture must take into account that the board's overriding concern was moderation in design.

A distinction must be made between Fair-built structures (those erected by the Fair corporation for the focal exhibits of each zone and for rental to prospective exhibitors) and private structures (those erected by individual exhibitors). The first category usually was more conservative in design than the latter, which had generally more spontaneous visual and structural effects. In both categories, the objectives of variety and unity were critical factors, thus determining the general character of architectural design at the Fair. Within them at least three stylistic strains were evident: the first already has been termed Beaux-Arts moderne; another concerned the expression of the building's purpose stylistically; the third was based on the imagery of streamlined forms. Although these strains were not mutually exclusive, for the sake of clarity they are presented below separately.

Fair-built Structures and a Beaux-Arts Moderne Style

The design board specified certain requirements for the construction, materials, plan, and aesthetics of the Fair-built structures, the first to be erected. Among its specifications were mandatory steel frame construction surfaced with gypsum board and stucco; a standardized cubic unit of 20′ dimension for all exhibition spaces; the location of main exhibition spaces at ground level; the prohibition of neon signs and red lighting; and a maximum height of 15′ for the signs that would identify the exhibitors. Departures from these standards involved occasional changes in materials or construction techniques but not in the aesthetics of advertising. Fair-built structures were variations of six basic building types devised by the design board. The board's idea was that elements of like character placed in each zone of the main exhibit area would provide a unifying context for the buildings to be erected later by private exhibitors. Because they were an indication of the design board's effort to discourage elements which might have disrupted the desired harmonious effect, the Fair-built structures were considered to be the backbone of the Fair.[19]

So it was that certain commonly recurring features of the Fair-built structures set the tone of the exhibition: low extended façades of single-story height; colonnades both straight and semi-circular; exedrae; rotundas; cupolas; domes; and the accentuating masses of towers, pylons, and pyramidal units. Large stretches of windowless wall were commonly given over to exterior murals or to concentrations of sculpture or ornament. Façades were colored in bright hues or given visual interest through the skillful use of fluorescent, flood, and neon lighting; various materials (glass, ceramics, wood, metal, and the new synthetics) were employed for their inherent qualities of color and texture. Structures rather dull in composition—the Communications Building, the Home Furnishings Building, the Metals Building, the Business Systems and Insurance Building—were contrasted to those which were exploited for their sculptural effects—the Electrical Products Building, the Hall of Pharmacy, the Hall of Fashions, Food Building Number 3, the Home Building Center, the Contemporary Arts Building. At some buildings—the Consumer's Building and its antithetical neighbor, the Building of Science, Medicine, Public Health and Education—movement was directed around ample court spaces by means of a series of changing elevations.

The Fair-built designs ranged from uninspired to imaginative and were, in differing degrees, variants of Beaux-Arts classicism. Besides the standard repertory of columns, domical forms, tower-like masses, and the like the structures frequently bore classicistic ornamental motifs, such as bandings and fluted surfaces and their compositions were typified by stark juxtapositions of simple geometric units of hierarchical groupings.

Neoclassic idioms were joined with mural art, sculpture, and the contemporary Art Deco taste for ornamented and colored surfaces. The combination yielded what could be called a synthetic Beaux-Arts moderne style. Occasionally, this Beaux-Arts moderne style was found in buildings constructed by private exhibitors, two significant examples of which were the American Radiator Company pavilion and the Schaefer Center. A dominant note is sounded: appeal to the public through a variety of styles within a framework of classicism.

Fair-built and Private Buildings and the Symbolic Expression of Purpose

One major indication of the design board's influence is a mode of imagery which, evident in at least two Fair-built structures, was adopted voluntarily for private buildings. The imagery resulted from the board's contention that a building's exterior shape should symbolize its content and purpose.[20]

That a building should "speak" of its intended function through its form was the theory of *architecture parlante*, postulated by the romantic-classic architects of late eighteenth-century France. By taking up this idea, the design board maintained its ties with a Neoclassic tradition associated with rational design and sanctioned an architecture which, through its imagery, could inspire immediate public recognition. Exemplary of *architecture parlante* was the Fair-built Marine Transportation Building, which signified its purpose by a gigantic pair of oceanliner prows and a 150-foot mast. Avoiding this obvious mimicry, another Fair-built structure, the Aviation Building, evoked the spirit of flight by means of a conically-shaped hall that suggested a wind tunnel or a hangar. Although their obvious shapes distinguished the Maritime and Aviation buildings from other Fair-built structures and each other, they were comparable in that their compositions of large, simple, sculptural forms created an immediate impact on the beholder. The use of *architecture parlante* allowed the board of design still another way of obtaining qualities of free expression without giving up traditional notions of architectural logic and order.

Several other buildings used *architecture parlante* to direct attention to a company's commercial product or industrial activities. A powder box shape signified the Cosmetics Building unmistakably. The Petroleum Industry Building was an impressive triangular structure resting on four oil tanks with a full-scale moving oil derrick to one side. The Railroad Building, the largest structure at the Fair, featured an eight-story rotunda intended to evoke a roundhouse. A giant igloo advertised the Carrier Corporation air-conditioning exhibit. A number of buildings had more obscure shapes which had emanated from the blueprint stage. The R.C.A. Building, for example, was described as shaped like a giant radio tube, and the Gas Exhibits Building's 90-foot-high ceremonial pylons, placed radially in a Court of Flame, were said to resemble gas burners.

Likewise the Continental Baking Company Building was likened to a doughnut, although immediate recognition of the company's product was ensured by the Wonder Bread wrapper motif of red, blue, and yellow balloons that covered the curved entrance façade. Literal product symbolism was most blatant in the over 40-foot-high National Cash Register pavilion. Surmounted by the "world's largest cash register," whose function was to total the daily attendance at the Fair, the pavilion was banished to the Amusement zone for failing to respect the requirements of decorum of the main exhibit area.

Towers and domes provided additional means of symbolizing commercial and industrial enterprise. Clustered in the vicinity of the Plaza of Light, the towers and domes were variations of the Trylon and Perisphere forms north of the plaza. To signify its theme of harnessing electricity to serve man, the General Electric Company created a lightning-bolt-like tower topped with an astrolabe. As a symbol of electrical energy, the entrance court of the Electric Utilities Building displayed a 150-foot-high transmission tower of open steel framework. The staid, 108-foot-high rectilinear tower of the Glass Industries Building demonstrated the practical use of glass block. By contrast, the dramatic Westinghouse tower, 120-feet high, was a looming inverted cone of six concentric rings held by steel rods. The 105-foot-high Du Pont tower was a skeletal construction, research apparatus suspended within it. The Westinghouse ring-tower drew attention to where the Fair's famous Time Capsule was buried while the Du Pont tower, with its surrounding exedra of open steel framework, alluded to the company's advances in chemistry.

Domes were fewer in number and in general were not as memorable as the towers. In keeping with the Fair's atmosphere of quick changes in mood and message, the Elgin pavilion's astronomical observatory, signifying the measurement of time by the stars, was located next to the Carrier pavilion's symbolic igloo. Of greater interest than either of these two buildings was the dome of the U.S. Steel pavilion. The hemispherical dome was an overt expression of both structure and form. Sheathed in stainless steel and suspended from external steel trusses, the dome symbolized steel's structural and decorative possibilities. Its strikingly formal qualities contrasted sharply with the nearby beehive dome of the Heinz pavilion which featured a unique method of thin-shell timber construction, surfaced over to create a neutral field for the mural art that projected the message of the exhibit. Neither the domes nor the towers were marvels of structural engineering—their significance lay in the skillful use of materials, color, innovative lighting techniques, and vivid shapes used to advertise commercial and industrial ideas through futuristic images.[21]

Streamlined Form: Symbol of a Machine Age

Although the Fair's architecture was calculated to entice the public into the various exhibits, it sought also to create a fantasy environment that would evoke its planners' vision of the industrial democracy of the future. The towers, pylons, fins, domes, and the arc-like and serpentine roofs punctuating the skyline at irregular intervals were forms intended to spark the belief that a better tomorrow was within everyone's grasp. Architecture and art were united to celebrate the new age of the machine, the admired new child of science, industry, and business. The rhythmic pulse and vitality of the new technological age was to be embodied in another pervasive symbol—streamlined form.

All types of structures at the Fair employed the rounded contours and smooth surfaces of streamlining. Streamlined form, by about 1930, had come to be associated with the Art Deco or moderne style, popularized by architectural and industrial design. Streamlining was applied to airplanes, automobiles, and ships for greater speed, to machines, as a visible parallel to movement, and to static forms such as architecture and product design for harmony of shape and outline.

Two of the most elegant applications of streamlining were the Bridge of Tomorrow, which connected the Fair's Administration Building with the main exhibit area, and the bridge-like Long Island Rail Road station. The Bridge of Tomorrow conveyed a sense of movement with a series of parabolic arched steel trusses, which supported a gracefully curved roadway and roof. The railroad station itself, a timber and canvas structure supported by five transverse arched-steel trusses, was an elaboration of the covered bridge idea. A curved roof with flush, band windows provided smooth enclosure with the appearance of a streamlined railroad passenger car. Two entrances to the Fair, the separate Corona gates of the Transportation zone, were each flanked by imposing pylons of diagonal and rounded contours, emphasized by linear bands. The streamlined forms that swept the visitor into The World of Tomorrow became a leitmotif of the Fair.

Several buildings used streamlining to convey an idea of aviation and flight. One section of the Firestone Building was shaped like the tapered outline of an airplane body and tail fin. The sleek smooth surfaces and border fins of the elongated Swift and Company building suggested a super airliner. Unlike the Aviation Building itself, where, paradoxically, streamlined forms conveyed the idea of air flight without overt references, neither the Firestone nor the Swift buildings had anything to do with expressing the immediate function of their respective companies. Indeed, so popular and compelling was the streamlined image of flight that an early issue of the *New York World's Fair Bulletin* likened the Fair's radiating avenues to an "airplane in silhouette."

Streamlined forms were also the distinctive marks of the Ford and General Motors buildings, two of the stars of the Fair in terms of both their exhibits and their architectural conceptions. Arch competitors in the automotive field, the two companies sponsored buildings which seemed to highlight the corporate differences through diametrically opposed expressions of movement and sculptural massing. The Ford building was composed of a changing rhythmic sequence of elements that featured a garden court and an open-air theater, with a triple-tiered spiral ramp leading to the elevated Road of Tomorrow. By contrast, the curved walls and rounded parapets of the General Motors building created a series of seamless enclosing shells, the shapes of which were determined by the location of the

Marine Transportation Building. (PMW)

internal displays and by the intricate circulation pattern. Within a cool, inward-turning container, the General Motors Building moved people on a journey through Futurama, a city as it might appear in 1960. At the Ford building, a demonstrative display of the highway and the automobile was achieved through the technology of reinforced concrete. The vigorously curved and angular forms were quite the opposite of the General Motors Building's calm stretches of vertical and curved wall planes, enhanced by the metallic glow of lacquered surfaces.

Both buildings were the result of a collaboration between the same architect, Albert Kahn, and different industrial designers, Walter Teague for Ford, and Norman Bel Geddes for General Motors. In each case, the industrial designer's role seems to have been a major factor in determining the result. In the Ford

structure, the display was dramatically extended to the outside; in the General Motors Building, it was expanded within delimiting walls. Their co-existence at the Fair illustrated the variety of ways in which streamlined forms could serve different functions.

Streamlining was an outgrowth of the clear geometry and control of Neoclassic form. It embodied as well those ideas of Neoclassic theory that dealt with symbolic expression in design. Thus streamlined forms had a place in the classicizing structures of the Beaux-Arts moderne style—the Sealtest pavilion, for example—as well as in structures that exemplified the symbolic notions of *architecture parlante*—such as the Aviation Building.

There were distinct precedents for streamlining in exhibition architecture. Two early twentieth-century designs, the Austrian Josef Olbrich's Plastic Arts pavilion of 1901 at the Artist's

U. S. Steel Building. (PMW)

Colony in Darmstadt, and the Italian Raimondo d'Aronco's project for the Automotive Pavilion at the 1902 Turin Exposition of Decorative Arts, had expressively used contour and surface to symbolize modernity. The German Eric Mendelsohn applied streamlined forms in sketches and executed buildings of the teens and twenties, some of them for exhibition buildings. Foreshadowing the Fair planners, Mendelsohn had used streamlining as a way of conveying a sense of life rhythms along with the dynamics of modern industry. By the early 1920s, Norman Bel Geddes's spectacular architectural projects had helped to popularize streamlining in America. In an important breakthrough for an industrial designer, a number of his projects were proposed—though not executed—for the Chicago fair. At the Fair, streamlining became a major ingredient in the shaping of architecture in the service of advertising.

Long Island Rail Road station during Fair construction, late 1938. (HB)

MODERNE versus MODERN:
DECO versus INTERNATIONAL STYLE

Critical reaction to the Fair's architecture was largely unaccepting of its hybrid and blatantly commercial character. The diversity of architectural forms and effects had been explained by Fair officials as a "reflection of our own day in its complete lack of period style."[22] Those critics who reviewed the Fair, however, were not prepared to accept an architecture of advertising and industrial styling in any sense.

Although the terms deco and moderne that are in vogue today were not employed as such to describe the Fair's architecture, their features were clear, and clearly disliked by the critics of the time. Commentators wrote of the architecture's "decorative touches," and of its superficial "modernity."[23] The architectural critic Talbot Hamlin, writing in *Pencil Points*, referred to the spurious effects of "modernist"[24] detailing and diagnosed the curvilinear, streamlined forms to be symptomatic of "attacks of acute circularitis or spiralitis."[25] Architectural qualities were

examined by Frederick Gutheim not for their symptoms but for the cultural cynicism they revealed. He charged that the Fair buildings revealed a licentious liaison between architecture and big business for the blatant purpose of advertising and sales. If a single style had been generated, he concluded, it should be called the "Corporation Style."[26]

Given this outpouring of displeasure, it is well to remember that the Fair's architecture—with variable effects of structure, color, and ornament—stood in direct opposition to the mainstream of 1930s avant-garde modern architecture, the International Style. Unlike the Fair's popular modernist designs and their "bundles of tricks,"[27] the International Style was regarded as the objective canon of modern devices and ideas. The only Fair buildings that were praised in the critical literature were those that could qualify as modern within these rigid limits, and this category was comprised almost exclusively of pavilions sponsored by the foreign governments of Argentina, Brazil, Finland, Sweden, and Switzerland. Of all the architecture at the Fair, it is these designs that have been given the most study for their original interpretations of modern principles. For the rest, only occasional

structures and exhibit displays were commended for their design qualities—among them the previously mentioned Aviation Building, the stainless steel umbrellas of the E.G. Budd Manufacturing pavilion, the Hall of Democracy inside the Pennsylvania State pavilion, and various Fair-built shelters, light standards, information booths, and souvenir stands. But within the vast exposition, these represented only a tiny proportion. The general opinion, which has survived into the present, was that the architecture at the Fair offered "little of significance."[28]

The Fair's architecture deserves to be reappraised for exactly those qualities that placed it outside the canonical International Style, for they pointed the way to a revision of our expectations concerning architectural form and meaning. The Fair's pejoratively called Corporation Style—in which color, lighting, and bold, sometimes delightfully bizarre forms, were employed to mythologize business's and industry's role in the shaping of America's future—offers an excellent perspective from which to begin; its innovative design aspects prefigure the architectural redefinitions that have taken place in America during the last twenty-five years. The Fair's architecture combined elements of the popular deco style with the traditional arts, and joined them with the devices of industrial design and commercial advertising to create an exposition architecture of wide public appeal. Its success in this endeavor was uneven, to be sure, and the result was often a curious blend of social idealism and crass commercialism. Nevertheless, the Fair displayed an architecture whose sculptural, pictorial, and ornamental effects exceeded anything that had been produced in America or Europe up to that time. It provided a major source for significant new directions in American design. A telling expression of our cultural aspirations at the end of a disastrous decade, it marked the beginning of a renewed quest for a world of order and reason.

Brazil (Oscar Neimeyer Soares and Lucio Costa, architects). (PMW)

NOTES

This essay is intended as an introduction to some of the broad aesthetic and social issues raised by the architecture and planning of the 1939/40 New York World's Fair. My purpose has not been to analyze single structures in detail—with the exception of the Theme Center and, to a lesser extent, the Ford and General Motors buildings. Nor have I been concerned with the particular orientations of architects, architectural firms, and industrial designers, or with the character of two of the special areas of the Fair, the "Town of Tomorrow" and the Amusement Zone. It is anticipated that these and other aspects of the Fair will be examined in a subsequent publication.

Working with Helen Harrison, guest curator of the exhibition, has been a delightful and rewarding experience. Janet Schneider and Shelley Grossberg of the Queens Museum have continually provided expert guidance and criticism. To Sara Blackburn go my deepest thanks for her sensitivity and insight in helping to bring greater clarity to my essay. Terrence Jablonski has seen me through every stage of the project, and he alone knows what this has meant to me.

1. "Fair of 1939 will depict the 'World of Tomorrow,'" *The New York Times*, October 9, 1936, p.1.

2. See John G. Cawelti, "America on Display: The World's Fairs of 1876, 1893, 1933," in *The Age of Industrialism in America*, ed. Frederic Cople Jaher (New York, 1968), pp. 317-363.

3. See "Information from Modern Movements seen in Architectural League," *Art Digest*, v.11 (1 May 1937), pp. 5 and 29; Peyton Boswell, "The World of Today," *ibid.*, v.13 (1 June 1939), p.15; Talbot Faulkner Hamlin, "The Architectural League Exhibition," *Pencil Points*, v.19 (June 1938), pp.342-356.

4. "World Fair Friends Rally to Keep 'Parthenon off Flushing Swamp,' " *New York Herald Tribune*, December 12, 1935, p.26, cols.2 and 3; *The New York Times*, December 12, 1935, p.33.

5. See *The Fair of the Future 1939*, a Proposal submitted by the Committee Formed at the Dinner at the City Club, Wednesday, December 11, 1935; Amended February 10, 1936, p.20.

6. Reported in *The New York Times*, May 22, 1936, p.25, col.2 and May 23, 1936, p.14.

7. *New York Herald Tribune*, December 12, 1935, *op.cit*. For Teague's influence in promoting the theme of the future see "World's Fair, New York Style," *Business Week*, September 28, 1935, p.18.

8. Quoted in *Architectural Forum*, v.65 (December 1936), Supplement, p.8. For provisions of the competition see, "Competition for the design of a typical building," *Architectural Record*, v.80 (December 1936), pp.462-464, and "New York Fair Competition," *Architectural Forum*, v.65 (December, 1936), Supplement, pp.8, 41.

9. Twenty-three winning projects were published together with brief criticisms by Kenneth Reid, "World's Fair Competition," *Pencil Points*, v.17 (December 1936), pp.655-677; for further discussion of the competition see my "The 1939 New York World's Fair Three Years Before; Controversy and Architectural Competition," *Arts Magazine*, v.52 (November, 1977), pp.108-112.

10. See "Robert (Or-I'll-Resign) Moses," *Fortune* 17 (June 1938) p.138, and Robert A. Caro, *The Power Broker: Robert Moses and the Fall of New York* (New York, 1975), pp.1082-85. See also Gilmore D. Clark, "Landscaping," *Architectural Record*, v.84 (November 1938), pp.97-98.

11. S.F. Voorhees, "Adapting Plans to the Site," *Engineering News-Record*, v.121 (September 22, 1938), pp.357-358 and *idem*, "Circulation," *Architectural Record*, v.84 (November 1938), pp.99-100.

12. On the plan see Talbot Hamlin, "World's Fairs 1939 Model," *Pencil Points*, v.19 (November 1938), pp.672-686. See also "The New York World's Fair—its Theme and Plan," *American Architect and Architecture*, v.149 (November 1936), pp.44-45, and Richard Kent, "World's Fair at New York: Its Theme and its Designers," *Pencil Points*, v.17 (November 1936), pp.609, 619.

13. See for instance *New York World's Fair Bulletin*, v.1, no.6 (June 1937), p.2, also New York World Fair 1939 Department of Feature Publicity, *Painting and Sculpture in the World of Tomorrow*, n.d., p.4.

14. See "World Fair Urged to Drop Old Idea," *The New York Times*, May 28, 1936, p.25, and "Toward Fairer Fairs," *American Architect and Architecture*, v.149 (July 1936), pp.53-56.

15. H.R. Hitchcock, "Paris and Flushing: Sober Thoughts about Twentieth Century Expositions," *Shelter*, v.3 (April 1938), pp.38-45.

16. "Board of Design contacts Harrison and Foulhoux to design 'Theme Building,' " *The New York Times*, November 25, 1936, p.16, and *Architectural Record*, v.81 (January 1937), p.7' "Floating Sphere to Dominate Fair," *The New York Times*, March 16, 1937, p.25.

17. See "World's First Spherical Building," *Engineering News-Record*, v.101 (August 30, 1928), p.331.

18. New York World's Fair 1939 Department of Feature Publicity, *op.cit.*, p.7, *Official Guide Book: New York World's Fair 1939* (New York, 1939), pp.20-21.

19. See R.H. Shreve, "Design of Exhibit Buildings," *Engineering News-Record*, v.121 (September 22, 1938), pp.369-374.

20. On this policy see *New York City World's Fair 1939 Information Manual*, February 25—"Architecture," n.p.; also *Official Guide Book: New York World's Fair 1939*, p.20.

21. See Walter Dorwin Teague, *Design This Day: The Technique of Order in the Machine Age*, New York, 1940, *passim*, on the contribution of the Fair to architectural design.

22. *New York World's Fair 1939 Department of Feature Publicity*, *op.cit.*, p.7.

23. "Review of 1939 New York World's Fair," *Architectural Review*, v.86, *op.cit.*, pp.55, 62.

24. Talbot Hamlin, "The Architectural League Exhibition," *op.cit.*, p.348.

25. "World's Fairs 1939 Model," p.676.

26. Frederick A.Gutheim, "Buildings at the Fair," *Magazine of Art*, v.32 (May 1939), pp.286-289; 316-317.

27. Talbot Hamlin, "The Architectural League Exhibition," *op.cit.*, p.355.

28. Paul F. Norton, "World's Fairs in the 1930's," *Society of Architectural Historians-Journal*, v.24, (March 1965), pp.27-30

Eugene A. Santomasso is Assistant Professor of Art and Architectural History at Brooklyn College and at the Graduate Center of the City University of New York.

General Motors Building. (NYP)

THE FAIR PERCEIVED:
Color and Light as Elements
in Design and Planning

Helen A. Harrison

The monumental, almost overwhelming scale of the 1939/1940 World's Fair makes it difficult to appreciate the fact that it was essentially a collection of individual exhibits, all of which competed with one another for attention. The Fair's effectiveness and influence therefore depended upon easy access to the exhibits; they were, after all, the concrete demonstrations of how visitors could perceive the sponsors' ideals of progress and future material prosperity.

The responsibility for developing a general site plan that would allow the visitor to find the exhibits with a minimum of confusion fell to the Board of Design, the seven-member committee that was also to arbitrate in matters of architecture, landscaping, and exterior decoration. The board studied the layouts of previous fairs, consulted with various architects and designers, and discussed numerous plan proposals in an effort to achieve unity and intelligibility. The plan they finally adopted—the wheel, or radial arrangement, with avenues extending like spokes from a central hub—was presented in July 1936 by architectural consultant William Orr Ludlow and Hugh Ferriss, one of the board's official architectural delineators.

Advance publicity promoted the radial plan as the ideal solution to the chronic fatigue that had plagued visitors to past expositions, almost all of which had been far smaller than the "World of Tomorrow." *The New York Times* predicted that "it will be an easy Fair to look at and get around in. The many diagonal streets and the grouping of exhibits save legwork. Intramural

buses, tractor trains, taxi-chairs and push-chairs reduce the strain for the foot-weary."[1] But the plan was not without its critics. Talbot Hamlin, the distinguished writer on architecture, expressed sentiments that many Fair visitors would echo when he complained that the several entrances to the grounds and the tendency of the magnetic Theme Center to draw pedestrians to its surrounding courtyard would have a *dis*orienting effect. "Just how the crowds pouring into this circle from so many directions are to know which way to turn and *how* to get *where* is still an interesting question," he wrote in late 1938, when Fair construction was well on the way to completion.[2]

A DREAM OF FAIR COLORS

One device chosen by the planners was to color-code the Fair, according to a plan devised by Julian E. Garnsey, a muralist and former consultant to the Texas Centennial Exposition, where a tawny color scheme had been used to reduce the glare of the Dallas sun. The idea's most notable precedent was the 1933/34 "Century of Progress" exposition in Chicago, where architect Joseph Urban had developed a color scheme to guide visitors by reflecting the moods of various exhibits. Although Urban's scheme was later described as spotty and ineffective, the concept of color as an orientation device was still considered feasible. The Fair's *Official Guide Book* noted that a new and cohesive approach to color-coding had been adopted, resulting in "a harmony previously unknown in any great exposition."[3]

Consultant Ludlow had suggested that color could serve an orientational function when he wrote to the board of design in support of his radial plan, maintaining that order could be achieved by "each spoke identifying its particular kind of exposition by designating colors for each, displayed by flags by day and colored lights by night."[4] But Garnsey saw the potential beyond Ludlow's flag concept and suggested imposing a spectrum format on the Fair's semicircular plan. Working with Ernest Peixotto, president of the National Society of Mural Painters and a consultant to the board, Garnsey found that a rainbow of shades could be superimposed easily on the existing layout. "They tried it on a miniature model, stood back, and blinked. Here was something. Then they set to work," the *Herald Tribune* reported. The newspaper described the resulting color scheme as follows:

> At the axis of the design, trylon and perisphere stand in pure, dazzling white, flanked by a softer "theme white" on the adjacent facades. From the theme center the colors undergo a gradual transition along the avenues which radiate from it like spokes from the hub of a wheel. Along the Avenue of Patriots a gamut of yellows shade from pale cadmium to deep gold at Bowling Green. Down Constitution Mall the progression is from rose to burgundy, and a series of blues on the Avenue of Patriots culminates in ultramarine at Lincoln Square.
>
> Connecting the ends of these vistas, Rainbow Avenue curves in an arc from gold through orange to red, and on through violet and blue. Within this frame of color lie the buildings, each related to its neighbor and to the whole.[5]

The guide book made a particular effort to alert visitors to the color scheme and to make them aware of its potential value as an orientation tool. It explained that some sixty-five buildings in the main exhibition area fitted into this color plan. "Relations between adjacent and successive buildings have been arranged to present exciting and inspiring experiences in color perception," it stated earnestly. "Walls of daffodil yellow are broken by vermillion pylons, purple buttresses appear against rosy domes, and vistas of turquoise blue terminate in great ships' bows of ultramarine." However, visitors were assured, large areas of off-white wall were provided to alleviate the possibility of "fatigue of color impression."[6]

Buildings in the Government sector were graded delicately in tone from creamy white (the United States Building at the easterly end of the Court of Peace) through seven shades of closely related values, ending in rosy gray. This graduated tonality provided transition to the strong reds of the Food zone buildings at the end of Constitution Mall. It was further stated that "optical effects are used to heighten color effects. At the entrance to the Golden Plaza, for example, blue violet light in the Long Island Rail Road Station prepares the eye for the flash of complementary golden yellow seen immediately afterward."

Exterior mural decorations were keyed to harmonize with and incorporate the predominant color schemes of their respective zones. Thus Philip Guston's sophisticated figurative compositon for the main entrance façade of the WPA Building was set on the yellow ochre background characteristic of the northerly Avenue of Patriots. In Carlo Ciampaglia's murals for the Food Building, a female figure representing natural bounty floated on a field of brilliant red, indicating a central position on Constitution Mall. The huge curving wall complementing the flowing, organic forms of Willem deKooning's semi-abstract mural on the Hall of Pharmacy was electric blue, an indication that the building was on the Fair's southerly axis. (Green, notably absent from the planner's decorative spectrum, was supplied in abundance by the landscape plantings and by the 10,000 full-grown trees that had been transported to the site during the three-year reclamation project.)

Appropriately separated by the Grand Central Parkway from the main body of the Fair, the Transportation zone was not keyed to the color scheme; rather, subdued tones and shades of off-white gave the buildings a cohesive quality that emphasized the sculptural mass of these largest exhibits. The General Motors, Ford, and Chrysler pavilions were predominantly eggshell white; Firestone, Goodrich, and the adjacent Railroads Building had color schemes of soft yellow, rust, and tan. The Aviation Building, hangarlike in shape, unabashedly displayed the natural colors of its asbestos and canvas sheathing. The exhibit of the Budd Manufacturing Company used unpainted stainless steel to great advantage. Only the Marine Transportation Building on the southernmost edge of the zone sported a brightly painted façade, adorned with twin ship's prows (each thirty feet taller than the bow of the *Normandie*) in ultramarine blue. This building also boasted a handsome and predominantly blue mural of abstract ship motifs by the recently repatriated modernist Lyonel Feininger, a long-time resident of Germany and former Bauhaus instructor.

Like the radial plan, the Fair's color scheme served theoretically to insure the swift orientation of visitors and to help them perceive the themes of the different zones. In practice, however, Fairgoers either entered with a preplanned itinerary (easily devised with the aid of the massive and sustained pre-Fair publicity) or wandered randomly in search of interesting or amusing exhibits. The colorfully decorated façades provided excellent subject matter for Kodachrome snapshots and the newly popular home color movies, but they did not succeed in impressing visitors with an underlying rationality. Few visitors were aware that the Fair's use of color was actually an ingenious orientation plan.

Visitors were not likely to be enlightened about the color-coding on a typical trip to the Fair. Most of the buildings used the colors assigned to them only as decorative relief on their entrance façades, or as backgrounds for their murals, leaving the majority of wall-surfaces uniformly creamy-white. The summer glare heightened the predominant whiteness, and so did the sun-bleached plaster of the numerous monumental sculptures that were placed at key intersections.

Viewing the grounds from the bridge between the Trylon

(Architectural Forum)

and the Perisphere—at a height of sixty-five feet, the most elevated vantage point accessible to the public in the radial section of the Fair—visitors saw, rather than the color-coded walls of buildings, the luxuriant foliage of the trees lining the five broad avenues that radiated out from the Theme Center. Indeed, it seems that the only way to appreciate, or even to notice, the spectrum effect was by viewing the grounds from the air, a vantage point available only to passengers on flights to and from nearby La Guardia Airport and to crews of the blimps that frequently hovered over the site. The painstakingly planned color scheme was not even evident from the 250-foot high crown of the Parachute Jump in the Amusement zone.

"It was a good idea—especially on paper," wrote one commentator, "but when a couple of hundred designers, corporation presidents—and their wives—give it a going over . . . what have you got? As near as we could figure out, you've got a pretty random batch of hues doing a darn good job of surprising you, jolting you, pepping you up, wherever you walk. It's the old circus idea of color—with a college education."

No effort was made to color-code the Amusement zone, where a carnival atmosphere prevailed. "Here, color drops its Harvard accent and lapses into pure unadulterated circus," it was said. Garish billboards and arresting façades proclaimed the wonders of the girlie shows, burlesques, and the oddities designed to shock, titillate, and entertain the masses. Some attractions had

educational pretensions—the Music Hall, with its program of symphonic concerts, the mock village of Merrie England, complete with a replica of the Globe Theatre, and the Theatre of Time and Space planetarium—but most were unabashedly in the side-show tradition.

Morris Guest's Little Miracle Town, a Lilliputian world inhabited by seventy midgets who could be observed at simulated work and play, was entered through a false front adorned with a huge mural caricaturing famous stage and screen personalities. The Dream of Venus, a pavilion designed by the Surrealist artist Salvador Dali, was decorated with the heads and bodies of outlandish aquatic creatures, and visitors bought their tickets from a booth set between the legs of a fantastic female sea monster. Dancers jitterbugged on a balcony outside the Savoy Dance Hall. With each amusement competing with over one hundred others for attention, and survival depending on the brisk sale of tickets, provocative exteriors were the order of the day.

In his press releases and public statements, Grover Whalen, the Fair's president, included the emphasis on color in the list of the expositions's futuristic aspects, noting that he expected the actual world of tomorrow to be a colorful one. Whalen felt that, as the 1893 World's Columbian Exposition had popularized neo-classicism in American architecture, so the Fair would promote chromatic enrichment. "It will make people demand color in their cities just as they now demand color in their kitchens and bathrooms and clothes. They will insist on brightening up the drab surroundings to which we have all become accustomed," he wrote.[7]

The Fair was not to exert the chromatic influence Whalen foresaw. The postwar ascendency of the so-called International Style in urban architecture—characterized by clean unbroken surfaces, the use of monochromatic skins of glass and metal, and the elimination of decorative detailing—shows that the corporate sector, at least, was not inspired to fulfill his prediction. It is reasonable to surmise that in the minds of both the exhibitors and the public, the bright hues and striking decorations applied to Fair buildings were analogous to product packaging, for commercial and industrial interests have traditionally sought the contemporary equivalent of classical decorum for their permanent structures.

LIGHT AS DESIGN AND MAGIC

The 1939 first edition of the *Official Guide Book* introduced the subject of the Fair's miracle of light thus, on page 39:

> Visible for miles around, a flood of multi-colored light drenches the sky above the glowing spectacle that is the Fair at night. Light, fire, color, water, and sound have been ingeniously and subtly blended to create a dazzling scene that embraces every band of the spectrum . . . . The city of magic, it might well be called, an enchanting vision hinting at the future in artificial illumination.

The Fair's theatrical use of color was more intensely apparent at night when buildings radiated from concealed lighting sources that either enhanced their daytime colors or imbued them with a dramatically different chromatic effect. External floodlighting was discouraged, and most exhibitors successfully incorporated their lighting as an integral element in the design of exteriors and interiors. The board of design regarded the development of innovative uses of light, much as the myriad applications of color, as one of its abiding concerns. To serve this end it hired a battery of consultants on electrical engineering, pyrotechnics, industrial design, and architecture, headed by electrical designer Bassett Jones. As reported in the magazine *Movie Makers*, the consultants took the bit between their teeth. "We're all crazy as loons," Jones was quoted as saying, "but there's never been anything like it before."[8] An early plan, subsequently abandoned, involved the idea of incorporating fluorescent substances in the exterior wall-paint and activating it at night by ultraviolet radiation to transform the walls themselves into sources of illumination.

Floodlighting was restricted to the Theme Center, where a series of spectacular effects transformed the Perisphere into the world's largest movie screen. As night fell, the globe was bathed in colored lights—first amber, then deep red, and finally an intense blue—on which were superimposed moving white lights (filtered through mica) in irregular patterns, simulating clouds. Placed on rooftops 250 feet or more from the building, projectors were so

accurately focused that no "spill" effect was discernible. Unlike ordinary floodlighting, this technique produced "a great pattern in living color . . . that will make its appeal because of its magnitude and sheer beauty."[9]

The result bore an uncanny resemblance to the views of Earth which would be taken from Apollo spacecraft some thirty years later and also served to mask the unfortunate surface irregularity of the Perisphere's otherwise pristine geometry. The sphere specialized in providing unique projections for special occasions: at a Fair preview to mark the birthday of Thomas Edison (February 11), a seventy-five foot portrait of him was projected on its surface; for Independence Day, a red, white, and blue light pattern transformed it into a patriotic backdrop for the sixty-five foot statue of George Washington in the center of Constitution Mall; and, on Hallowe'en, closing day of the first season, it became a giant orange jack-o'-lantern.

Even the drabbest and most monochromatic of buildings sprang to life under the influence of creative lighting techniques. By day, the only touch of color that relieved the honest metallic finish of the U.S. Steel dome was the minimal application of blue paint to the external ribs that acted as its structural supports. But by night, the ribs glowed a bright azure that the shiny steel surface reflected, and the entire dome gleamed with a cool radiance. The tower of the Glass Industries Building, lighted from within, exploited the translucency of glass-brick and the blue of plate, becoming luminous at night, acting as a beacon, and attracting attention from great distances.

Buildings with unusual and popular daylight features rose to splendor at night.

Italy's pavilion, featuring a 200-foot cascade of water descending in three stages over its façade, used submerged lateral projectors and interior lighting to make the water sparkle and dance, an effect that delighted countless nighttime visitors. The waterfall covering a wall running eighty-five feet along the exterior of the Electric Utilities Building was illuminated in pure white by the use of high intensity mercury-vapor lamps. By day the wall of water had a cool and shimmery aspect; at night it was transformed into a curtain of liquid crystal enhanced further by the deep blues and greens of the adjacent walls.

Concealed lighting strips along the guard railings of Ford's Road of Tomorrow highlighted the novelty of the new multicolored Fords, Lincolns, and Mercuries which wound around the building's spiral ramp in an endless procession, seeming almost magically animated.[10]

The Columbian Exposition had introduced the public to incandescent lighting on a civic scale, the Century of Progress fair had been the occasion for the first practical, large-scale demonstration of neon tube lighting, and the World of Tomorrow showed that the newly-perfected fluorescent light was both effective and versatile.

According to the magazine *Electrical Engineering*, "the Fair served as a stimulant to creative minds seeking departures from the conventional; also as a proving ground for new and better light sources, for improved methods, systems, and techniques. Its success is evidenced by such developments as the rapid commercial acceptance of the low-voltage fluorescent lamp and the increased consciousness of lighting as an element of architectural design, a foretaste of the practices of tomorrow."[11]

Exhibitors made wide use of both low- and high-voltage fluorescent tubing, either hidden in coves and recesses or open to view, used as sculptural elements in design. It was fluorescent light that made the ribs of the U.S. Steel dome glow at night, and that provided the backlighting for countless mural sculptures, decorative plaques, and illuminated signs, creating color accents on otherwise monochromatic walls. One of the most spectacular applications was the design of the Petroleum Building, a triangular-plan structure featuring fins of corrugated steel ascending its outer surface in four concave strips. Behind each strip a trough containing blue fluorescent tubes produced indirect illumination that made the building's horizontal segments seem to float independently in space.

Fluorescent lighting was frequently incorporated in the free-standing pylons, information booths, and street lamps that punctuated the Fair's avenues and acted as guideposts for visitors. At the Corona Avenue entrance gates two sets of twin sixty-six foot streamlined pylons welcomed Fairgoers to the Transportation zone; they were particularly dynamic at night, highlighted by recessed strips of fluorescent tubes. The graceful "hairpin" pylons outside the Hall of Special Events were designed by Nembhard Culin, a board of design employee who also created many of the Fair's other lighting fixtures. For the dramatic hairpins, Culin ran pink and green fluorescent tubing in a wave pattern over laddered steel frameworks.

Polarized light provided some of the Fair's more unusual decorative accents, even being incorporated into one of its artworks. An animated mural by Henry Billings, commissioned by the World's Fair Corporation, occupied the central position over the entrance to the Transportation focal exhibit, in the building which housed the Chrysler Corporation display. Because of the dual functions of the pavilion, the mural inevitably was associated with Chrysler.

During the day, the mural appeared as a translucent glass panel containing the abstract forms of a streamlined automobile, a comet with flaring tail, a diagrammatic drawing of an internal combustion engine, a star containing a gear symbol, and a planet form with a symbolic speedometer. When lighted, however, it became a mobile pattern of shifting prismatic color, which was effected by means of rotating discs of wrinkled cellophane and polarizing plastic and a stationary polarizing disc.[12]

Animation by means of light, often coupled with other spectacular effects, was a guaranteed crowd pleaser. At the Westinghouse Building, for example, the Singing Tower of Light put on a popular show that included color changes and flashing rings of illumination, and which was climaxed by the release of water, smoke, and fireworks—all to a musical accompaniment. At the General Electric display a steel fountain imitated the flash of a lightning bolt. Over the entrance to Du Pont's Wonder World of Chemistry a 100-foot sculptural construction resembling

laboratory apparatus seemed to bubble and glow with experimental chemical substances being demonstrated in the company's exhibit. A ballet of dancing water jets, designed by Alexander Calder, added another dimension to the fountain-covered blue-glass façade of Consolidated Edison's City of Light. Nozzles hidden under the Perisphere released gas flames and spurts of water that made the massive globe appear to float on a spectral cloud.

Every night at 9:00 p.m. the Lagoon of Nations—the oval reflecting pool that separated the Government zone from the rest of the Fair—was the scene of a sound and light display of unprecedented magnitude. Under the direction of Bassett Jones, who was assisted by John Craig, an expert on pyrotechnics, Joseph Jarrus, a gas engineer, and a team of technicians, the fountain spectacle employed over 1,400 water nozzles and 400 gas jets; it was illuminated by a three-million watt lighting system, with 585 colored drum lamps and five giant spotlights, supplemented by 350 firework guns. The entire display was set to music, broadcast by four stereophonic amplifiers located within the lagoon. A symphonic band, playing in a studio some quarter mile distant, provided the accompaniment. Three technicians coordinated the effects from a console in the U.S. Government Building. The average cost was $1,000. for each show.[13] (see page 51)

The displays were designed by Jean Labatut, Professor of Architecture at Princeton University, and they featured such predictable themes as The Spirit of George Washington, Fire Dance, Isle of Dreams, and Creation. Labatut gave his sketches to the composer Robert Russell Bennett, who provided appropriate scores to harmonize with the visual effects. John Craig developed special noiseless fireworks so that the pyrotechnic display would not interfere with the musical accompaniment.[14] This spectacle, far surpassing the complexity and magnitude of the sound and light displays at previous fairs, was immensely popular and provided a dramatic and attention-getting climax to what might well have been a day of aimless rambling. For those hardy souls who gravitated to the Amusement zone after the closing of the main fairgrounds at 10:00 p.m., there was a larger, and some said more impressive, sound, light, and fireworks display (also designed by Labatut) in Fountain Lake at midnight.

As described by Gretl Urban, a Fair music consultant, the Lagoon of Nations display was designed as "a new type of esthetic expression for a popular spectacle . . . based on visual architectural expressions—color and form. Music was then composed . . . as for a choreographic composition, but, this time, the dancer is not man, but matter, with water, light, gas-flame, and fireworks taking part."[15] In a somewhat less esthetic spirit, the show was described by Fair publicists as "the nearest approach to chaos that man can contrive for purposes of sheer entertainment."

Both technical and popular publications made much of the accomplishments of the engineers who created the Fair's spectacles in light and color. Inventors and designers from the commercial world, given a free hand and a generous budget, let their imaginations run riot. "Their only thought for the consumer was to knock him off his feet," wrote one enthusiast. "It was an

Petroleum Building—day (PMW)

engineer's utopia . . . . They made models of their displays and then had to dismantle them because everybody stopped work to watch the models. Whatever they did was done with an eye to color. They wallowed in the spectrum."[16]

The approach succeeded, for the sound and light displays and, indeed, all of the lighting effects, drew universal acclaim. One survey of exhibition techniques concluded that the Fair's imaginative use of light was its most notable contribution to exposition design, the "most effective device for playing on the emotions of the spectators, to put them in a receptive frame of mind, to quiet them, to stimulate them, and generally prepare them for the exhibits."[17]

In accord with their generally sober and moralistic attitudes toward the purpose and message of the Fair, the planners viewed the more spectacular aspects of display with some trepidation. In its September 1936 report to the committee on Physical Planning,

the board of design warned that exterior illumination should be strictly controlled. "The night lighting of the Fair should be dignified and derive its interest because of its beauty and splendor rather than because it is a spectacle of theatrical effects," the report advised. "It should in the main have a character and quality expressive of future possibilities rather then merely attempt to exaggerate a scheme of illumination that has been commonly used and developed in the fairs of the past twenty years."[18]

In his generally harsh and disapproving criticism, Talbot Hamlin compared the lighting of the World of Tomorrow unfavorably with that of the much smaller and less diverse Golden Gate International Exposition in San Francisco, which ran concurrently with the Fair during both its seasons. Hamlin contrasted the quality of the Fair's night illumination with what he described as San Francisco's "carefully composed, exquisitely colored harmony." Nonetheless he was forced to concede that the

Petroleum Building — night (GK)

Lagoon of Nations displays were something San Francisco—and indeed no other fair—could touch. "These deserve to be called examples of a new art, and the best of them . . . are as emotionally moving as they are visually exciting," he wrote.

The *Fontaines Lumineuses* at Paris in 1937 showed some of the possibilities for beauty in the controlled motion of water under changing color, but there was about them something basically indecisive and unsatisfactory; one felt a lack of rhythm in their changes, a lack of inner artistic cause. The addition of music has, in the New York displays, superbly filled this need and given firmness and structure to them; . . . they have given the New York Fair its most unique and perhaps its most artistically memorable element."[19]

Ultimately, the Fair's lighting managed to serve the ends of both idealists and pragmatists. The variety bespoke the imaginative genius of its designers; the architectural applications brought out the character of buildings and sometimes changed their forms, endowing many of them with far more interest than they could claim in their naturally illuminated states; the symbolic functions were exploited effectively; and the technology was innovative and fascinating both to the specialist and the layman. For the thousands who went to the Fair only in the evening and for those who spent all their time in the Amusement area, the dream of Fair colors was a dramatic and memorable reality.

INTERIORS: LIGHT AS TEACHER AND SEDUCER

When we consider how much of our life comes to us through our eyes, how light governs the very pattern of our being, the dominant significance of lighting in exhibition design becomes readily apparent. The part it plays is subtle and many sided; its influence on the mood of the spectator can hardly be exaggerated.[20]

Intriguing, expressive architecture, enhanced by decorative color and innovative lighting effects, was, of course, only the seductive icing on the cake that was the real substance of the Fair: the exhibits. Inviting the public to take a bite was the function of this packaging, just as the volumes of advance publicity and advertising were designed to stimulate attendance. The official and commercial exhibitors both had something to sell. For the former, it was the ideology of planning, interdependence, and enlightened technological development promoted by the Theme Center and focal exhibits; for the latter, it was their wares. Each group influenced the other in the planning phase. Under the watchful eye of the board of design, the Fair was prevented from becoming a crassly commercial jumble of merchants' blatant advertising, while the Fair planners took a leaf from the merchants' book and employed the sophisticated talents of the industrial and commercial design world to good effect, if not to the same ends.

Even Robert Kohn, chairman of the committee on theme and one of the key theoreticians of the Fair's socially-oriented planning, was quick to realize and acknowledge the more mundane appeal of such an exposition. In October 1936, at a conference where he addressed a discussion group of twenty-four representatives of the city's cultural institutions and interested individuals, he announced that:

> the Fair is based on the idea that this is what a business man called a "consumer's fair," . . . oriented toward the non-technical person, . . . in terms that could be understood by the average person, so that this average visitor to the Fair could find something . . . which would mean something in his own life . . . . That is the theme with regard to everything, for the average, ordinary folks who come to have a good time. Something which means something to their lives and which they can have if they go after it.[21]

Kohn's acknowledgement of the superficiality upon which fairs are generally predicated did not prevent him from seeking earnestly to impress visitors on a more sophisticated level. He probably did not realize that, when he spoke of what folks can have if they go after it, he was in fact describing the material offerings of General Motors, RCA, and Westinghouse, rather than the intangible social values of his own pet project, Democracity. Still, he was aware that drama and the inspiration of awe through the medium of effective exhibit design were as much a part of a successful educational exhibit as of a commercial one.

Democracity itself was an excellent example of the application of the most advanced design techniques to convey a non-commercial message, and much of its appeal was in the special effects of its lighting and projections. Like the Lagoon of Nations spectacle, it was a multi-media event that depended on the interaction of the latest and most complex components of sound, light, and animation. During a program that took the visitor through a simulated twenty-four-hour cycle in the life of Democracity, the city of 2039, the planners' ideology was communicated largely through the use of novel and impressive lighting techniques.

During the daytime segment of the cycle, strips of lamps concealed behind the rotating observation platforms of the Perisphere flooded the dome with blue light and the effect of moving clouds. Similar to the building's nighttime exterior, this created the impression of a natural sky. As evening fell, the blue deepened to midnight and stars appeared. (The planetarium was still in its infancy, so few visitors were familiar with such effects.) Then ultraviolet lamps, hidden under the lower platform, acted upon touches of fluorescent paint on the model landscape below, picking out "lighted" windows, highways, and other details. This black light provided the model's only illumination during the night sequence. As darkness came to Democracity and its satellite towns, the dome of the globe became a screen for the projection of the propagandistic sky mural thrown by ten specially designed Kodak drum-gear projectors. These carried glass slides portraying groups of united citizens marching toward a common and harmonious future. The entire show, including lighting changes, vocal narration, slide projections, and musical accompaniment, was automatically synchronized.

Writing in *Movie Makers*, Loran Harrison noted that "when the images fill the dome, the screen surface is an acre and a quarter! It is the equivalent to a theatre-height screen two thirds of a mile long." The glass-mounted 35-millimeter Kodachrome slides were projected in sequence, giving the illusion of forward motion by means of dissolves and the gradual increase of image scale. For the finale, polarizing filters created a "crystal curtain" that spread to cover the dome's entire interior surface with prismatic light.[22] Early technical problems produced some instances of daytime narration playing at night and the occasional loss of vocal and musical tracks, but the difficulties were evidently ironed out by the end of the first season. In spite of its teething troubles and a hefty 25¢ admission charge, the Perisphere attracted over 5.7 million visitors during 1939.

In his plan for the interior of the Perisphere, Henry Dreyfuss, Democracity's designer, had intended to incorporate a "blaze of Polaroid light" as the apotheosis, but technical problems in the development of the necessary equipment appear to have forced him to adopt the less dramatic device of polarizing slides. This must have been a frustrating disappointment, because the concept of light as a medium of expression had played a significant part in his initial planning of what was the Fair's key thematic presentation. He wrote, "my first impulse was to have something abstract—a great light effect, brilliant colors moving over form, a show of magnificent movement, color and excitement—" but this plan, like dozens of other fanciful schemes, was ultimately abandoned in favor of a more concrete expression of the "Interdependence of Man."[23]

All of the Fair-built buildings and most of the commercial and government exhibits used artificial illumination for their

The Lagoon of Nations. (NYP)

interiors, and this allowed a far greater degree of control over color effects than did natural light. It gave designers not only a means of focusing attention, but also a flexible tool for establishing and varying mood.

The General Motors Futurama, the vast, imaginative vision of motorized America of 1960, magically combined many features that made it an odds-on favorite at the Fair, but it was more than content that insured its appeal. A study of the Fair's exhibition techniques singled out the *lobby* area of the Futurama ride as an especially effective lighting and sound environment that eased

visitors into a receptive frame of mind after their long, fatiguing wait on line outside the building:

> To prepare the visitor for the Futurama he was led through a dim, blue lighted room. Here his attention was arrested by an enormous map of the United States, silhouetted in the darkness. On it a network of illuminated lines appeared by stages, showing our present highways in relation to the traffic they carry and how they might develop in the next twenty .

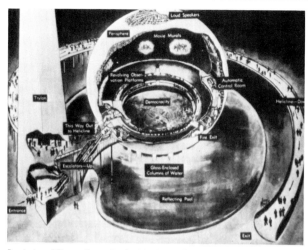

Rendering of Theme Center focal exhibit, Henry Dreyfuss, designer. (HAH)

years. Out of the darkness an unseen voice, pitched in a low key, described the effect of the highways on the growth of the country and explained the significance of the future changes which flashed on the map. The darkness helped to fix the visitor's attention and the pitch and tempo of the voice lulled him into a receptive mood.[24]

The study concluded that the relief of sinking into the cushioned seat of the moving chair-train that carried spectators on a one-third mile simulated air trip across the country (as remade to designer Norman Bel Geddes's specifications) was the "final touch" in this skillful build-up." By contrast, the panorama itself was naturalistically lighted, with day and night cycles similar to those in Democracity, but without the symbolic use of special effects.

Also naturalistic but nonetheless dramatic was Consolidated Edison's City of Light, publicized as the largest diorama (perspective model) ever built. The model, a scale replica of the New York skyline, with the Hudson River and New Jersey shore visible in the background, was lighted and animated to illustrate the applications of electric power in modern urban life. Spectators stood in a viewing gallery where the model, designed by Walter Dorwin Teague, occupied a semicircular wall. As they watched darkness fall on the homes, shops, factories, and docks, a narrative "voice from the sky" described the throwing of the switch that flooded the city with artificial illumination. "This is the City of Light, where night never comes . . . . a world of power at the motion of a hand."[25] Cutaway sections showed power surging through underground mains, voices speeding across miles of cable, electrified subway trains moving the city's work force, the instantaneous broadcasting of information by radio and telegraph, and many other aspects of urban life that depend on a ready supply of energy. Even the natural drama of an electrical storm was portrayed as a challenge to the resourcefulness of the power

company, which would heroically respond to provide an increased supply of energy during the daytime darkness.

The Electric Utilities exhibit, sponsored by a consortium of light and power companies, featured modern illumination as the star of its show. Visitors were taken on a tour of a dingy street of the 1890s, when gas, kerosene, and oil were about to give way to electric lighting. After passing through displays that illustrated the development of new lighting techniques, they emerged into the Avenue of Tomorrow, where glass-fronted shops, offices, and apartments radiated the even, glareless glow of the very latest in lighting technology. In the adjacent Chamber of Light, a sculptural arrangement of crystal forms acted as the focal point of a light, color, and music display of psychedelic proportions.

Several exhibitors exploited the light-transmitting properties of the newly developed synthetic plastics, including Du Pont's Lucite, Plexiglas by Rohm and Haas, and the phenolic resins. To represent the twelve sectors of its display on the functions of government, the United States World's Fair Commission decorated the federal exhibit with nine-and-a-half foot cast resin statues lighted from inside the bases; these dramatic, glowing accents symbolized such themes as National Defense, Education, Social Welfare, and Conservation. For the Winthrop Chemical display in the Medicine and Public Health Building, a life-size "transparent girl," equipped with concealed lighting at strategic points, demonstrated the effects of anesthesia upon the human body. In the same building, the focal exhibit by Ian Woodner-Silverman made use of a life-size male figure in transparent plastic, complete with internal organs, to reveal the "hidden facts of human anatomy." For the focal Communications exhibit, designer Donald Deskey created a twenty-foot plastic head representing Man the Communicator. A light source within this transparent sculptural construction projected images to the far end of the darkened hall; a voice narrated the history of communications.

To illustrate the light-carrying properties of Plexiglas, Rohm and Haas installed an animated display in its exhibit in the Hall of Industrial Science. One commentator described how, by pushing buttons in the display, "lights of various colors and intensity play upon the hidden ends of pieces of Plexiglas. This illustration shows how Plexiglas can both 'pipe' light around bends and curves and how it can intensify light by bringing it to a pencil point."[26] Such effects, familiar today, were unprecedented at the time of the Fair. In the view of Robert Gaston Herbert, a model maker who helped fabricate plastic components for General Motors's Futurama, the manufacturers of these revolutionary plastics did not yet know themselves just what could be accomplished with their materials, so they welcomed experimentation. Rohm and Haas even sponsored a competition for sculptors to develop artistic applications of Plexiglas; the first prize went to Alexander Calder.

Clear plastic was used to great advantage as a dramatic substitute for the opaque coverings that normally hide the inner workings of mechanical devices. Crowds flocked to see the transparent Pontiac, constructed by Fisher Body, in the General Motors Highways and Horizons exhibit. "This car is complete with

Workmen put the finishing touches on the model Empire State Building in Con Edison's "City of Light." (WDT)

Transparent car by Fisher Body for General Motors Exhibit. (HAH)

windows which can be raised and lowered, doors that can be opened and closed," wrote one admirer. "It might be driven out on the highway should occasion demand."[27] And appreciative audiences gathered in the lobby of the RCA Building, where a transparent television revealed the perfection of cathode ray transmission.

Television itself, although it had been under commercial development for some ten years prior to the Fair, was a novelty to the American public. In fact, regular programming had been instituted in Britain in 1936 and experimental stations were operating in the United States before 1939, but it was not until the Fair that average Americans were presented with television's potential as a medium of communication and entertainment. Broadcasts from the RCA, Westinghouse, and General Electric exhibits, as well as mobile camera units set up around the grounds, motivated Fair visitors to speculate whether television would one day replace radio as the focal point of millions of American homes. David Sarnoff, President of RCA, felt confident not only that the "living room of tomorrow" would be fully equipped with the electronic means to receive television and short wave radio, but also that recent strides in microwave transmission would enable the broadcasting of radio signals to automobiles. "If we go a step further," he postulated, "we may visualize motorists in separate cars talking to each other as they speed along the highway."[28] Clearly, in respect to broadcasting, the World of Tomorrow heralded the dawn of a new day.

The Fair's use of light as a tool for motivation and influence was also apparent in the showplace it provided for film. Over 600 motion pictures were screened during its two seasons. They ranged from the abstract color evocation of flight by animator Len Lye, in the Science and Education Building, through a multitude of travelogues and documentaries, to the patriotic pastiche, *Land of Liberty,* assembled by Cecil B. De Mille out of footage from some 124 feature films and 100 newsreels for the United States Government exhibit. What follows is a brief view of the most innovatve technology and design that used projected imagery as its medium.

"For sheer delight, fantasy, mystification, and sustained interest, Chrysler's ten minute Polaroid three-dimensional motion picture was one of the high spots of the New York Fair," the survey of exhibition techniques announced.[29] The film, *In Tune With Tomorrow,* depicted the various parts of an automobile arranging and organizing themselves into a finished car, in time to

music composed by George Steiner. The components were photographed in stop-action by two cameras set at divergent viewpoints corresponding to the two slightly different angles of human vision. By viewing the film through special polarizing glasses, with each lens admitting only one of the two viewpoints, a naturalistic, three-dimensional Technicolor image was created. As the car parts danced into place, the concept of automation took on a new and magical meaning.

Film was the ideal vehicle for the combination of entertainment, education, and product promotion that made up most of the Fair's commercial exhibits. In assessing the effectiveness of the various displays, *Exhibition Techniques* stressed the importance of a balanced presentation: "If the Fair had been advertised as an educational project and if people had the feeling that they were going through an educational process, the exposition would have had far less popularity. It was this procedure of educating while entertaining which made the Fair the great attraction that it was." It was also noted that "there was a strong tendency to hold in check the strictly commercial aspects of displays. Exhibitors use the more round-about educational approach which in the long run proves both more worthwhile to the sponsors and decidedly more interesting to the public."[30]

Thus, in such films as *In Tune With Tomorrow* and Joseph Losey's *Pete Roleum and his Cousins,* which used animated plasticine puppets to tell the story of the development of the oil industry (and marked Losey's directorial debut), the promotion of the product was subjugated to the marvelous technical effects, trick photography, and entertainment value of the film itself.

In the Eastman Kodak Building, the Hall of Color amazed visitors with a panoramic mural of changing transparencies that ran for 187 feet around the semicircular hall. Each image was an incredible 22' by 17'; groups of slides illustrated such photogenic subjects as flowers, animals, and scenery. A continuous sweeping panorama of Bryce Canyon at sunrise dissolved into full daylight and sunset, followed by eleven static views. The entire cycle, lasting ten minutes and accompanied by music and narration, used over 2,000 separate 35-millimeter transparencies. Eleven giant projectors with twin drum-gear slide mounts were specially developed for this installation; for the mural to be effective on so large a scale, it was crucial that the slides be held rock steady and in perfect focus.

"They do it so perfectly, and the optical system is so skillfully constructed, that no eye can detect that the resultant image is not cast by a single beam from a single machine," wrote one observer.[31] Kodak's own publicity described the Hall of Color as "the greatest photographic show on earth," but hastened to point out that it was "all projected from transparencies such as you can make with any good miniature camera loaded with Kodachrome."[32] The message was communicated to the individual viewer on a soft-sell basis in an effort to make him feel he belonged in the exciting and progressive World of Tomorrow.

It is one of the Fair's many striking cultural indicators that it was the first exposition to be recorded naturalistically on film. Thus its color scheme and mural decorations—so much a part of its planning and design—and such a frequent focus of discussion among both enthusiasts and critics—have been preserved in photographs, transparencies, home movies, and color newsreels, and its spectacular fountain displays, innovative architectural and decorative lighting effects, and some of its dramatically illuminated interiors, can be experienced effectively in retrospect. The more stable photographic emulsions introduced in late 1939 aided in the preservation of true color, so we need not rely on descriptions alone to assess the impact on the popular imagination of the Fair's light and color.

The planners, architects, artists, designers, and engineers who created the World of Tomorrow drew on the era's most sophisticated technologies from the realms of art, industry, and commerce, synthesizing a vision of the future that was above all charged with energy—from the individual initiative and drive of the average consumer/citizen to the vast resources of power needed to fuel the world of Futurama, Democracity, and the Avenue of Tomorrow. In the face of the increasingly threatening international situation, the promotion of progress and optimism required an appropriately vivid setting. The Fair's dynamic application of color and light generously provided it.

Helen A. Harrison, the Guest Curator for this exhibition, is an art historian who specializes in American art of the 1930s. She writes on art for the Long Island section of *The New York Times*.

NOTES

1. "Here is the Fair," *The New York Times*, April 30, 1939, p. 3.

2. Talbot F. Hamlin, World's Fairs 1939 Model," *Pencil Points*, November, 1938, p. 675.

3. *Official Guide Book* (first edition, 1939), p. 37. (*Guide*).

4. Papers of the World's Fair Corporation, Manuscripts and Archives Division, New York Public Library, (*Papers*). Undated letter, Ludlow to Frank [Voorhees], presumably written in June or July of 1936. Box C1.0 (Board of Design) file: Ferriss, Hugh.

5. "Adventure in Pigments," New York *Herald-Tribune*, April 30, 1939, p. 39.

6. *Guide*, p. 38

7. Quoted in "A Dream of Fair Colors," John O'Reilly, *Movie Makers*, June, 1939, p. 276. (*Movie Makers*).

8. Quoted in "The Fair's Great Shows," Loran Harrison, *Movie Makers*, p. 279.

9. "New York World's Fair to set new pace in Lighting," *Lighting and Lamps*, September, 1937, p. 35

10. Technical information on Fair lighting is found in *Lighting and Lamps, Electrical Engineering*, the *Journal* of the Illuminating Engineers Society (September, 1939) and the *Edison Electric Institute Bulletin* (March, 1939), among other publications. I am indebted to Eugene Santomasso for sharing with me his notes on some of these sources.

11. Richard C. Engelken, "Lighting the New York World's Fair," *Electrical Engineering*, May, 1940, n.p. (offprint); lent to the research project by Henry F. Brzezinski. (*Elec. Eng.*).

12. Department of Feature Publicity, New York World's Fair 1939, "Art and Industry at the New York World's Fair," p. 7. Mimeographed pamphlet. Lent to the research project by Peter Warner.

13. *Elec. Eng.*

14. Kenneth M. Swezey, "Fountains of Flame Played Like a Pipe Organ," *Popular Science*, August, 1939, pp. 48-51.

15. Gretl Urban, "The Universal Language," *Think* (1940), p. 37. Lent to the research project by James Kurshuk.

16. *Movie Makers*, p. 279

17. *Exhibition Techniques: A Summary of Exhibition Practice* (New York: Museum of Science and Industry, 1940), p 28. (*Exhib. Tech.*).

18. *Papers*, Report to the Committee on Physical Planning, 8-31-36. Box A1.13 (Board of Design).

19. Talbot F. Hamlin, "Some Fair Comparisons," *Pencil Points*, October 1939, p. 648.

20. *Exhib. Tech.*, p. 67.

21. *Papers*, excerpt from a verbatim transcript, Report on Art Conference, October 28, 1936, pp. 1-2. Box C1.0, file: Committee on Theme.

22. *Elec. Eng.*

23. *Papers*, Box C1.0, file: Dreyfuss, Henry.

24. *Exhib. Tech.*, p. 39.

25. "The City of Light," descriptive brochure (Consolidated Edison, 1939), p. 5. Donated to the research project by Consolidated Edison.

26. I.L. Cochrane, ed., *Display Animation 1939-40: The Yearbook of Motion Displays* (New York: Reede & Morton, 1940), p. 95.

27. Cochrane, *op. cit.*, p. 31.

28. David Sarnoff, "Radio Casts its Ray on a New Era—Television," New York *Herald-Tribune*, April 30, 1939, p. 28.

29. *Exhib. Tech.*, p. 66.

30. *Exhib. Tech.*, pp. 15-20.

31. Arthur L. Gale, "Kodak 'Goes to Town'," *Movie Makers*, p. 303.

32. *Movie Makers*, p. 306.

THE USABLE FUTURE:
The Role of Fantasy in the Promotion of a Consumer Society for Art

Francis V. O'Connor

> Masses of people can never find a solution to a problem until they are shown the way. Each unit of the mass may have a knowledge of the problem, and each may have his own solution, but until mass opinion is crystallized, brought into focus, and made articulate, it amounts to nothing but vague grumbling. One of the best ways to make a solution understandable to everybody is to make it visual, to dramatize it.
>
> *Norman Bel Geddes,* Magic Motorways *(New York: Random House, 1940), p. 4.*

The 1939/1940 New York World's Fair ended a decade that began with the stock market Crash of 1929. After the boom years of the 1920s, the bust of the 1930s had a profound sociological and psychological impact, aptly defined in the several meanings of the word depression. A self-reliant people could no longer trust in themselves or their institutions; a God-fearing people found themselves impoverished of their best evidence of virtue; a pragmatic people, at first fearfully, later resolutely, asked why. Having no clear understanding of the technical causes of their economic situation, they found fault in themselves and looked to their origins in the past for solutions. The resulting national retrospection has become known as "the search for a usable past."

Patriotism fed upon history when providence seemed to fail. But toward the decade's conclusion a new attitude had set in. Those intellectuals and entrepreneurs for whom the depression was an impersonal reality sought pragmatic solutions to the economic crisis. And they invested an enormous amount of faith, energy, and treasure in the seductive concept of planning. What they planned can be called a "usable future."

Agreeing with Freud that the Marxist concept of social leveling was an untenable illusion, though obviously sharing something of the idealist planning theories it bred, they projected the vision of a tangible future—just around the corner. As historians have come to see, the New Deal was devoted to the radical rejuvenation of capitalism, not to its transformation into the socialist system it often was accused of attempting to establish. By the end of the 1930s, before World War II intervened, our more

conservative doers and thinkers sought to induce the resurrection of capitalism by applying the wonders of science and technology to the everyday life of the people. Unlike those who sought in the past a pattern of moral purpose with which to redeem the Depression, the new technocrats promised a future of material plenty for the masses—one which would permit a richer, less onerous, more streamlined life for every citizen. This reinvigoration would be achieved by the wiles and seductions of advertising and industrial design. In this widespread campaign for economic recovery, the Fair was one of the most flexible devices available to industry by which the nation's "usable future" could be projected upon the American imagination. Like all effective advertising, it played upon the fantasies of the consumer. And at the Fair, one of the most important media for fantasy was, as we shall see, carefully planned art and architecture.[1]

A fantasy is a phenomenon of imagination—one might call it an illusion—which has the affect of reality in prompting desire and action. It is to be distinguished from the merely fantastic, in which affect inheres in what is immediately perceived as untrue, contrived, or unreal. Thus, when the fantasy of planning is mentioned here, it is to be understood as the projection of a pattern of order and purpose upon specific historic situations, intended to occasion a desired good. That certain solutions presented at the Fair may now seem to have been fantastic is a legitimate historical judgment; but the fantasies which impelled them must be respected for the facts of cultural sensibility that they were, and, in some quarters, still are. Thus the word fantasy is not used in this essay as a term of disparagement, but in a neutral sense to describe how men, under the pressure of certain complex circumstances, collectively projected a myth upon their situation and acted accordingly. If the term seems an awkward way of characterizing serious human enterprise, it might be remembered that cultural history is the recording more of myths than achievements. We live by the illusions of our imagination—and plan accordingly. But, as we shall see later, the more unconscious we are of our fantasies, the more we believe we act with scientific objectivity.[2]

There is no more efficient context for fantasy than a fair or festival, and a world's fair, set in a park of monumental modern buildings and grandiose vistas, of fountains and sculptures and murals and myriad lights, is the ultimate fantasyland. Earlier fairs had turned to the grandeur of antiquity to envision a myth of the ideal. At Flushing Meadow in the last year of the 1930s, a fantasy of an idealized past was rejected for a fantasy of the planned future.

The fantasy of planning is the creative illusion that order can be imposed on the usual chaos of people and things—with beneficial results for all. At its best, it is essential for the civilizing process; at its worst, it is the bane of human progress. Planning is always an idealist enterprise posing as a science, and it is always in some manner defensive of the planners' moral, social, economic, or political values. No enterprise demonstrates this throughout history more clearly than that of urban planning. From the moated and stockaded castra of the Romans and the city plans of the Renaissance to the more subtle defense mechanisms built into contemporary urban renewal schemes, planning is a means of ordering by exclusion. The hallmark of modern art was then, and is still, abstraction—that reduction to essentials which has characterized all styles and movements in the visual culture of the century. This is true of the high arts of architecture, painting, and sculpture, to the lesser arts of commercial and industrial design. Since all forms of artistic activity were exploited at the Fair to promote a merchant's vision of a profitable future, and since the modern concept of abstraction (whether called Moderne, Art Deco, or streamlining) dominated the visual ambiance of almost everything at Flushing Meadow, it will be useful to contemplate—in the abstract, as it were—the fantasies of modernist art before turning to its more tangible and problematic manifestations.

When one studies the iconography of nonreferential forms in modern art, it becomes apparent that they derive from one of two general mental processes. I call these processes Geometry and Geomancy to emphasize their human universality and to remove them from art-historical contexts, which distort their psychological meaning with irrelevant labels and personalities. Geometry (Greek for "earth" + "measuring") develops according to internally consistent rules of logic. It is the rigorous application of rationality to objective physical situations, a method of abstraction—of taking away extraneous data so that pure mental constructs can be dealt with efficiently. Geometry, then, is a means of ordering the chaos of nature. It is a mechanism of defense which

permits the fantasy of clarity to be imposed upon life's normal confusion of variables.

By geomancy (Greek for "earth" + "divination") I mean a method of conjuring what is most urgent at any given moment within the psyche without abandoning life's normal confusion of variables. It is the process of psychological projection upon a random situation with the purpose of opening what is unconscious to conscious inspection. Geomancy, then, is a means of unifying, at a specific moment, the psyche with natural circumstances. It is a mechanism of insight which permits a fantasy of meaning to be imposed upon a situation.

In terms of art, geometry is the means by which artists protect themselves from inner experiences they have learned to fear, by imposing an arbitrary order upon a carefully selected number of variables. Geomancy is the means by which artists risk exposure to inner experience they have learned to value, by letting such experience integrate an arbitrarily permitted number of variables.

The distinction between the *order* at the heart of geometry's fantasy of clarity and the *unity* at the heart of geomancy's fantasy of meaning is crucial for art. There is a world of difference between disposing variables according to a system and combining them into *one* entity. Geometry values clarity at the expense of unity; geomancy values meaning at the expense of order. Both are legitimate means of human coping. Both are capable of resulting in aesthetically pleasing works of art. Both have profound implications beyond art, for they motivate more than the mere shaping of paint and clay. Indeed, both geometry and geomancy are awesome in their ethical implications: to impose order and to achieve unity are attainments of considerably different moral magnitudes.

The awesome thing about geometry is that it simply has to be internally logical—true to its impelling axioms. Given a little distance from the source, and no reason to maintain a memory thereof, the enchantment of the resulting relationships in art can be as entrancing as any new affair of the heart. They resonate with "truth," seem unarguable, and provide a satisfaction not dissimilar from that proffered by sentimentality. There is thus little difference, on this level, between Bouguereau and Mondrian, between Norman Rockwell and Stuart Davis, between Andrew Wyeth and Frank Stella. They all provide total intellectualized *donnés* which seem to preclude the necessity for geomancy.

The awesome thing about geomancy is that it requires the participation of both the artist and the viewer and demands transaction of the spirit beyond scientific verification. The work of art here is engendered not by a process of planning a specific layout and, after careful adjustment of its various relationships, coloring it in. Rather, what is involved is a far more complex process of letting the medium take the lead in the image-making process. The ideal of the artist throwing down his marks upon the vacuity of the picture plane and giving himself totally to the extraction—the divination—of their particular meaning within the logic of his sense of form and symbol is a world apart from the artist who seeks consciously to plan a set of formal relations for its own sake.

And now let us ask why geometry is more effective as a medium of consumer formation than geomancy—why the Fair was a veritable monument to the reductionist aesthetics which were dominant after the first War, and which we will see to have been resurgent after the brief efflorescence of Abstract Expressionism.

The answer, I would suggest, lies in the very human fact that our modern consumer society is not capable of absorbing for its own sake an art committed to those qualities of feeling, emotion, intuition, and manticism which must inhere in any balanced and integral work. Planned people require art in their own image—which is why Jackson Pollock's apparently uncontrolled pouring technique was such a scandal until its results became a good investment in the 1960s. Having reluctantly given up the philistine desire for an art of narrative representation, art consumers wanted obviously contrived images to prove their stature as intellectuals, to give the appearance of being modern (rather than, merely difficult), and—clearly being planned upon the ever more sacred picture plane—to defend themselves against the terrors of accidental insight. In short, they wanted and got what bourgeois collectors have always got for their spare cash: clear, precise, narrative representation. And if depictions of people and things were unfashionable, then depictions of the axioms of anybody's new geometry would do.

The utility of geometric thinking is as a psychological defense mechanism. It requires only careful, neat planning, the playing out of whatever axioms a particular formal situation dictates. It efficiently masks the unconscious (which it denies anyway as an active force in art) by "willing" conscious contrivance to dominate the creative experience. Whatever is left of the geomantic sensibility is put to the service of order rather than unity—which results in psychological manipulation rather than growth. Nothing is left to the risk of imagination—and, at the expense of a fantasy of unity, the fantasy of order is maintained as a means of objective, unthreatening, intellectually seductive modernist expression for those who find it useful as a mechanism of advertisement and remuneration.

THE TRYLON AND PERISPHERE: THE FANTASY OF MODERN DESIGN

We perceive that the person who would use a machine must be imbued with the spirit of the machine and comprehend the nature of his materials. We realize that he is creating the telltale environment that records what man truly is . . . We are entering an era which, notably, shall be characterized by *design* in four specific phases: design in social structure to insure the organization of people, work, wealth, leisure; design in machines that shall improve working conditions by eliminating drudgery; design in all objects of daily use that shall make them economical, durable, convenient,

congenial to every one; design in the arts, painting, sculpture, music, literature, and architecture that shall inspire the new era.
Norman Bel Geddes, Horizons *(Boston: Little Brown, 1932), pp. 4-5.*

At no time was the Fair visitor denied the illusion of being immersed in total modernity. Awareness of each participating exhibitor's version was usually determined by the scale of the grounds. This kinesthetic experience of the Fairgrounds is important because it has much to tell about the twin modern fantasies of planning and design.

The pedestrian at the Fair, even though equipped with a map, normally could not feel the over-all coherence intended by the Fair's plan. Instead attention was paid to the curious edifice directly in view, to its landscaping, its lighting (if at night), one's personal interest in its subject, such as energy, automobiles, health, cows being milked, one's state or country of origin, etc. The elaborate color scheme (described elsewhere in this catalogue) was better in theory than in aspect, obscured as it often was by thick stands of trees. The various divisions of the Fair might be found on the map, but could not readily be felt at ground level. Only from the Parachute Jump and the Helicline could the "white city" of the Fair be glimpsed as a whole—and then only obliquely. Indeed, the planning and design of the Fair were conceived by men looking down at blueprints and models. As a geometric axiom, the Fair was brilliant in conception; as an environment, it was simply confusing. It was a fantasy of order, not of unity.

The Trylon and Perisphere at the Fair's center constituted the most avant-garde architectural design to be seen in its precincts. Heroically overscaled to dominate every vista, and painted the purest white in contrast to every other building on the grounds, this extraordinary megasculpture, by Wallace Harrison and J. André Fouilhoux, epitomized a vision of the future most other Fair structures only suggested as they struggled to exorcise the ghost of the Beaux Arts and earlier traditions.

The 610-foot high Trylon (its name a conflation of *tri* and *pylon* = a three-sided gateway) and the 18-story high, 180-foot-wide Perisphere (from *peri*: an encompassing globe) were embraced by the nearly 950-foot-long Helicline (from *helix*: a spiral incline) to create an overwhelmingly impressive proto-space-age primary structure with few precedents or successors in the history of architectural fantasy. Nevertheless, the Fair's president, Grover Whalen, chose to describe them in terms of historical styles, claiming the Perisphere and Trylon joined the "Greek idea of beauty of form and harmony with the Gothic conception of reaching ever upwards for a better world."[3]

Whatever the Gothic conceit (not to mention the equation of a better world with Deity), more to the point is the fact that the Fair's Theme Center required fractured Greek to articulate its futuristic tone to the pre-psychologized masses of the 1930s. Of all the past styles, that of the Greek seemed, in the public imagination, to embody the purity of style that industrial designers were eager to sell as streamlining. (That it did not is another matter entirely.)

Crowds enjoy the view from the Helicline. (AS)

Thus the chief theoretician of the Fair, Walter Dorwin Teague, in the epigraph to his 1940 book, *Design This Day,* quoted Socrates saying that absolute beauty was best found in "straight lines and circles, and the plane or solid figures which are formed out of them by turning-lathes and rulers and measures of angles."

That lathes, rulers, and protractors—basic equipment in anyone's incipient technology—should be the means by which the absolutely beautiful is attained says much about the rationalist reductionism at the core of Western presumptions concerning aesthetics. That these presumptions would be worked out to their relentlessly logical conclusions in that future designated "usable" is a major theme of this essay and will be discussed below. But let us examine what the generation of future artists was led to experience as the ideal of the NOW either as teenagers gawking at the Fair, through the media of the time, or through their parents' actions as modern consumers.[4]

The industrial designers who played so large a role in forming the Fair wrote passionately about the modern consumer. Couched in a language comparable to the dialogue in *King Kong* and certain scenes in *Citizen Kane*, their perfervid optimism reveals the hysteria of under-psychologized man: a childish boosterism that would return unconsciously to the order of the all-encompassing womb. The reversion leads to a level of fantasy that must consciously be denied in the name of hard-headed, machine-oriented rationality: planned order is the goal of design. According to Teague, design was "geometry made visible."

For the designer, geometry is the means to certainty and perfection. Teague's writing shows that he understood the dangerous allure of geometry; he knew that in spite of its "fascinating . . . narcotic . . . consuming" effect, "mathematical formulas never help a designer to create."[5]

For all his intelligent qualifications, Teague, and his colleagues insistently rationalized that somehow mankind's future redemption was at hand—through the resurrection of Platonic idealism, by recourse to the more recent theories of Jay Hambidge's "Dynamic Symmetry," via the pragmatic strategies of John Dewey, or by the indiscriminate application of streamlining. Their faith was not based on strict application of mathematical principle but on the moral conviction that the public good was to be attained by the universal adoption of a certain "rightness of form" in all matters, from the design of cities to the styling of pencil sharpeners. For design is geometry, and geometry is axiomatic ordering, and such planning is the source of certainty and certainty defends against the imponderables of life.

In the final analysis, streamlined forms served a more significant psychological function. A rounded exterior façade attracted attention to a building, but it also provided a sense of enclosure. However incomplete a curve, it invites completion. And inside a building, curving walls, often banded with polished metal, complementary bands of indirect lighting, luminous walls of glass bricks, their illumination so altered that it might have come from hidden electric bulbs rather than the sun, and the faint hum of ventilating equipment, all conspired to produce an impression of enclosing one in a totally controlled artificial environment. Future sets created by architects in the thirties reduced uncertainty nearly to zero. Although the association of streamlining with speed suggested endless progress into the future, its smooth forms also paradoxically suggested maintenance of static perfection.[6]

It was the Platonic fantasy of the industrial designers that there was but one perfect solution—one rightness of form—attainable for each problem in hand. This ideal soon was compromised by the industrialists' need for a new model each year; planned obsolescence soon did away with the uniqueness of a design as a single rightness. Thus, the industrial designers became the willing victims of that exclusivity at the heart of all planning which is a particularized reflection of the defense mechanism at the heart of the geometric fantasy.[7]

The lack of rightness in nature cannot be planned away. It must be faced, understood, and assimilated. The goal in any sane human enterprise is an ever-evolving integration of its diverse, and most often contradictory, elements. There is no certain solution; only such methods as an honest divination of the problem may prompt.

The industrial designers served best as the augurs of problems: even had they been able to do so, they had already sold their right to solve them. This goes for the designing of society as well as the designing of refrigerators. The industrialists had a far more psychologically sound sense of the real problem: human nature craves novelty, not elegant, static solutions. But the latent fascism of the designers, which allowed their compromises to co-exist with their visions, also fell in all too neatly with the political thinking of the optimistic capitalists of the day, who had yet to realize the danger brewing in Germany and Italy and were childishly fascinated by the psychological power of a modernized Greco-Roman aesthetic.

This fascination with the abuse of archetypes is a symptom of what I mean when I refer to the pre-psychologized mentality of the 1930s. While the American intellectual elite was actively aware of the implications of psychoanalysis and behaviorism by the 1920s, the American people were still unconscious of their unconscious. Freud was about sex and Pavlov was about drooling. As yet unconditioned to recognize unwilled motivations in themselves or others, the effect on their lives of consumer conditioning as conducted by psychologists employed by industry and advertising would be subliminal, to say the least. The paradigm of the application of psychological manipulation (or "humaneering," as it was called) to consumers was the presence of ex-Professor John B. Watson, the founder of American Behaviorism, on the staff of the J. Walter Thompson advertising agency. He had been set to codify "the laws of human reactions" of a "Mr. and Mrs. Consumer" as if they were mice or pigeons in a laboratory. The Fair was a carefully contrived conditioning experiment (Germany was another, at the time) and few among the multitudes entering its gates were ready in 1939-40—or subsequently—to "psyche out" the reasons they suddenly yearned for television sets, superhighways, foreign foods, and a streamlined life, or believed political and wartime propaganda.[8]

The Trylon was literally a huge needle, its eye the gateway to the Perisphere. Through the eye were threaded the hundreds of

Interior of Railroads Building. (LC)

thousands of visitors to the Theme Center. Entering up the world's longest escalator, they crossed the bridge which connected the Trylon to the Perisphere and exited down the Helicline. Inevitably the Trylon's height led the official guidebook to interpret it as symbolizing "the Fair's lofty purpose." (The stated themes were "Building the World of Tomorrow" and "The Interdependence of Man"—which might reasonably have been translated to "Commerce" and "Trade.") Certainly no one was going to remind the Fair's capitalist sponsors of the Biblical implications of needles.

Passing through the Trylon's eye was to achieve a vision of the future, one that was staged with all the bravura of a show at Radio City Music Hall. The Trylon's escalators deposited the public within the great globe on one of two circular platforms, which moved slowly in opposite directions. Below was a model of Democracity by Henry Dreyfuss, its periphery extended illusionistically beyond the moving platform to give the observer the sensation of floating in space. The lighting effect went from dawn to dusk in the five and one-half minutes it took to revolve the visitors back out through the Trylon.

A clever analogue to the Fair itself, Democracity was a great half circle centered on one imposing vertical skyscraper. It was designed to condition the visitor to the most basic idea the Fair was intended to convey subliminally: that it was, in itself, the center of the future. The future was NOW and it was around you as you walked down the Helicline. And you were at its center. The same device was used in General Motors' Futurama, which disgorged you onto the very street corner you had just seen close-up in the model.

Curiously static, sterile, and unreal, Democracity's vision of the future was a planner's version of regional suburban sprawl, a vast, Utopian stage set. The vaguely humanitarian ideals which inspired it were as psychologically and practically untenable as those of Marxism—as the history of the American suburb has amply demonstrated in the half-century since. It seemed to deny the existence of the poor, the incompetent, and the racially and ethnically dispossessed along with that midden of industrial and human waste dumped at the edges of any lived-in city.

Lest the visitors to the Perisphere think too much about these matters, they were distracted by continuous music in the form of a symphony by the black composer William Grant Still, over which the voice of H.V. Kaltenborn intoned a narration. The music, conducted by André Kostelanetz, eventually rose to what the guidebook described as "diapasonal" volume as processions of workers appeared from ten equidistant points on the interior dome. As this living mural approached to fill the sky, a choir sang an anthem by Al Stillman—the theme song of the Fair, the key verse of which was:

> We're the rising tide come from far and wide
> Marching side by side on our way,
> For a brave new world,
> Tomorrow's world,
> That we shall build today.

The Perisphere's spectacle concluded with a crescendo of sound and light, no doubt designed to obscure the anthem's unintentional reference to Aldous Huxley's 1932 novel, the plot of which might well have been staged within the well-planned limits of Democracy.[9]

This fantasy of the aesthetically pure, meticulously designed, rationally conceived "city of light and air and green space" was the central image of the Fair. The visitor, disgorged through the Trylon's eye to descend the embracing spiral of the Helicline, could see the Fair spread out in all its complex, classified glory. Unlike the Futurama exhibit by Norman Bel Geddes in the General Motors Building, which deliberately conditioned the visitor to the logic and necessity of superhighways (the better to create the political constituency to build them, the better to sell more cars), the Theme Center was dedicated to a moral rather than an economic imperative. It was the harbinger of the aesthetic life, in which everything was ordered, clean and neat, safe and efficient. In short, it was the purest distillation of the fantasy life of the un-psychologized post-Victorian middle class. And it was all contained in three overwhelming geometric forms which lent their power and drama to the fantasy in much the same manner as did the pylons, searchlight domes, serried phalanxes, martial anthems, and prophetic orations which, a few years earlier, had mesmerized the German nation to buy the fantasy of a thousand-year fate.

THE MURAL AS A MORAL FORCE: THE FANTASY OF ART'S REDEMPTIVENESS

> . . . a new art of design . . . accepts the characteristics of machine production not as limitations but as means for the creation of new types of rightness, and it sees the machines themselves as tools of enormously augmented effectiveness in the humanizing of our world . . . Obviously in this the designer is not a free agent. If he is any good at his work, he will not pluck his designs out of the air or out of the private storehouse of his invention. The imagination which makes him competent is not inclined to fantasy . . .
>
> *Walter Dorwin Teague,* Design This Day: The Technique of Order in the Machine Age, *New York: Harcourt Brace, 1940 p. 37*

While individual works of art, in all conceivable styles and media, abounded at the Fair, few of them proved memorable. The Fair itself made the lasting impression. Of the three divisions of the visual arts at the Fair—architecture, monumental painting and sculpture, and museum art—it was the vast array of modernist buildings which proved the most influential. Ranging from the futuristic spectacle of the Trylon and Perisphere, through the International Style street corner in the General Motors Building, to the Art Deco splendor of the United States Government Building, all the way down to the unprepossessing lumpishness of the Aviation Building, the architectural offerings at Flushing Meadow gave the public its first, concentrated experiences of that formal reductionism which was the hallmark of the modernity it was the Fair's purpose to market.[10]

The exhibitions of easel painting and pedestal sculpture, on the other hand, provided only cultural enrichment. Not surprisingly, they were an afterthought, permitted by the board of design only after insistent pressure from the press and public. Consequently, a Masterpieces of Art Building was allowed to be erected by private subscription, and it was filled with over 500 Old Masters from European and American collections which were selected by Dr. William R. Valentiner, director of the Detroit Institute of Arts. The Fair itself built a Contemporary Art Building containing twenty-three galleries with a combined 40,000 square feet of space. The irregular plan consisted of two rotundas connected by a series of galleries, the angles of which produced a zig-zag accent at the western end of Rainbow Avenue. In 1939 this building housed a large exhibition titled American Art Today, which had been assembled from all parts of the country. In 1940, in it were displayed, under the same title, a survey of over 800 works created nationally on the WPA Federal Art Project. Both exhibitions were strongly influenced by Holger Cahill, the WPA/FAP national director.[11]

During 1940, along with the Project exhibition, the Contemporary Art Building also housed the activities of a WPA/FAP Community Art Center, with working studios for arts and handicraft demonstrations, lectures, conferences, and performances. The WPA/FAP had established nearly seventy such centers around the country; the philosophy behind them was strongly influenced by John Dewey. They were devoted to the proposition that "participation in creative activity by the average person is of far more importance to the people as a whole than the passive appreciation of the work of a few exceptionally brilliant individuals."[12] Despite the project's idealist fantasy of art's social efficacy, and the virtue of planning they endorsed, the ideas which inspired the WPA/FAP nevertheless offered a direct challenge to the technological materialism rife at the Fair and recognized the consumer's cultural needs.

There were a number of other exhibitions at the Fair, such as the undistinguished show called Contemporary Art of 79 Countries sponsored by the International Business Machines Corporation in the Business Systems and Insurance Building. The works of art (one from each of the 79 nations) were intermingled tactlessly with the very latest business equipment in the spirit of a "come on"—a situation that did not go unnoticed by the critics of the day.[13]

There is little evidence that any of the large exhibitions, or any of the smaller collections to be seen in the foreign and state pavilions, had a cultural impact greater than that usually provided by New York's galleries and museums. Picasso's *Guernica*, shown at the Valentin Gallery in the spring of 1939, certainly had a greater impact on American art than anything the Fair offered. With the possible exception of the Trylon and Perisphere, the Fair's impact derived from its style and ambiance as a whole rather than from any single work of art.

Although non-objective geometric abstraction in the arts of painting and sculpture was the avant-garde of the 1930s, it was practiced by a very small number of artists. More prevalent were variations on Synthetic Cubism, which permitted a semiabstract montage style whose figurativeness was immediately seen both as modern and recognizably art. Most of the murals at the Fair were in versions of this moderne style. But the taste of the people was really reflected in the American Art Today exhibition, where regionalism and a tame social realism predominated. Thus nonobjective, geometric art was represented to the exact extent that it was tolerated in the visual arts of the time. It was, of course, tolerated when applied to architecture and industrial products because there it seemed practical, orderly, modern, and therefore, justifiable. But a pre-psychologized and undertechnologized culture was not yet ready to accept it as meaningful aesthetic expression.

The board of design commissioned 105 murals; many others were privately sponsored. The great majority were art-decoish academic decorations related more or less allegorically to the subjects of the buildings they embellished. Griffith Baily Coale's exterior murals for the Railroad Building are good examples of the type, with nude, stylized figures holding trains and surveying equipment. Less numerous, but of greater interest, were the abstract and semiabstract murals which presented avant-garde American art to the general public for the first time. These were almost all created by young artists who were, or had been, on the WPA Federal Art Project.

The most advanced murals by far were to be found in the Medicine and Public Health Building. The exterior walls of this edifice were painted with anemic academic visions by Hildreth Meière, the most sanguine being a vast depiction of "Mankind [a nude male] standing between the past and the future [i.e., the paws of the Sphinx] and looking [in the person of an enormous entity with streamlined hair] to the ever-advancing lamp of human knowledge for light."

Inside, the ever-advancing cause of art was represented by eight WPA Federal Art Project murals. The largest of these were by Abraham Lishinsky and Irving Block, and they consisted of two panels 70′ × 10′ and two 30′ × 10′, which depicted the history of medicine in a slightly retarditaire semiabstract Cubist montage style popularized earlier by Diego Rivera and Thomas Hart Benton. While this style was in itself radical in the eyes of the public, the four other panels, each 10′ × 16′ were far more stylistically advanced, two of them being totally nonobjective. These latter were by Ilya Bolotowsky and Balcomb Greene; the other two were by Louis Schanker and Byron Browne. All four were aptly described at the time as designed to:

perform the function of decorative visual spots in an interior filled with concrete realistic exhibits. Thus the visitor will come into the main entrance hall, see the large murals, study them as closely as he chooses and then turn into auxiliary galleries where he will experience the psychological relief of seeing large areas of color which do not demand close attention

but which afford an uncomplicated sensuous pleasure."[14]

Several other artists associated with the Project also painted major semiabstract murals for the Fair. Arshile Gorky designed a large wall for the interior of the Aviation Building, and Willem de Kooning and Michael Loew designed semiabstract murals for the exterior wall of Perylon Hall and the adjacent Hall of Pharmacy. Devastatingly, these murals, because of union regulations, had actually to be executed by members of the Mural Artists Guild of the AFL's United Scenic Artists and are thus hardly representative of the artists' best work. They did, however, introduce the public to a style of radical art not readily seen elsewhere.

Not surprisingly, considering the extent to which the last adherents of the American Renaissance mural movement of 1890-1920 had garnered mural commissions at the Fair, some of the best modern murals were to be found in the Works Progress Administration Building, where the WPA/FAP artists, with government assistance, joined the union in order to be free to paint their own walls.

The WPA building was intended to give the public a comprehensive view of the New Deal's work-relief programs. Although the Federal Art Project had been a miniscule part of the multi-billion dollar WPA effort since it began in 1935, it, along with the Federal Writers, Music, and Theatre Projects had in many ways defined the WPA's image in public awareness. Being controversial and conspicuous, the cultural projects were then, and remain today, indelibly associated with the Roosevelt Administration's battle against the human waste of the Depression. It is not surprising, therefore, that it was the Federal Art Project's murals which dominated the WPA building and, indeed, won two of the top prizes for murals at the Fair.

The titles of the major murals in the WPA building define the major areas of concern its various programs touched upon. The vast exterior mural by the future Abstract Expressionist, Philip Guston, was titled Maintaining America's Skills. Seymour Fogel created a large mural in the lobby on the theme The Relationship of the WPA to Rehabilitation. Eric Mose worked with the theme Building and Construction, which reflected the area of the WPA's most intensive activities. The distinguished textile designer, Ruth Reeves, executed a hand-painted mural-curtain for the auditorium, and Anton Refregier, a former associate of Norman Bel Geddes, painted eight tall panels on the Cultural Activities of the WPA.

Something of the artistic idealism of these young, radical, government-supported artists can be found in the following extracts from Refregier's diary.

JANUARY, 1939
The work is going full swing. The workshop is the closest to the Renaissance of anything. I am sure, that has ever happened before in the United States. My assistants and I have the central part of the studio. On the left, Philip Guston is working on the full-size drawings for the mural he is going to do for the

outdoor wall of the building. In front of us, Sy Vogel [sic]is working on a large canvas. In back, Eric Mose with his assistants. Other artists are working elsewhere. Every person here is dedicated to the Project. Everyone feels and knows that we must do our utmost. We know that there are a bunch of commercial mural painters preparing murals for the different buildings of the Fair—Hildreth Miere and others. They are making at least ten times more money than we are. But they can have it, Theirs will be the usual commerical crap. They are not moved as we are by our content—by our search for creative and contemporary design—by our concern for people. We are the mural painters. We hope we are catching up with our great fellow artists of Mexico. We will show what mural painting can be!!

APRIL.
The Fair is about to open. Today I was in Flushing Meadow to watch the installation of the murals. I have a feeling of tremendous satisfaction. I think we have done a terrific job. My design functions exactly as I expected. The execution by all the people involved is superb. I looked at the blue print beautifully rendered by the sign painter. The work of the other artists—Guston, Ryah Ludins—is superb. Our building is a gem and millions of people will see it.

MAY.
Harry Knight told me of an inquiry from Washington. A senator wanted to know if the figure of the immigrant writing the word "bread" on the blackboard had subversive implications. Son of a bitch! Damn right it is subversive! Let them eat cake![15]

Refregier's sense of the moral unity at the heart of his—and his fellows'—enterprise contrasts sharply with the ruminations of Stuart Davis concerning aesthetic order as a moral force, written as he planned his mural for the Fair's Communications Building. Davis, the country's most vocal proponent of abstract painting, was by far the most distinguished and sophisticated American modernist to contribute a mural to the Fair. He was a member of the Artists Committee which selected the 1939 American Art Today exhibition. His mural, sponsored by the Fair, was enormous: a 136-foot long, 44-foot high wall in the central hall of the building.[16]

During January 1939 Davis made a series of working notes about this mural which developed over the month into a draft essay. Immersed in the art and politics of his day, he was struggling to maintain the integrity of his abstract art in the face of increasing accusations of social irrelevance. His notes are of special interest because, with his Fair commission, Davis was faced for the first time since his youth (when he did a mural for a candy store in New Jersey, which looked not a little like some of the Fair displays [17]) with the creation of a commercial mural promoting the interests of a specific industry to the general public. A careful analysis of his evolving thought reveals that his attitudes in many ways anticipate the ideals of art twenty years hence, when he himself would be eclipsed by a new and more aggressive generation of formalist artists and critics.

In 1939 Davis would have strongly objected to being called a formalist, or to being associated with purely nonobjective, geometric artists. He refused to join the American Abstract Artists group because he felt geometric abstraction per se was meaningless and valued only by a cultural elite. He himself favored a semiabstract style in which recognizable objects were reduced to formal essentials and re-integrated into a Cubist pictorial space which he felt was "essentially an artistic reflection of the positive progressive fact of modern industrial technology." Yet this attitude was not very far removed from the industrial designers who ordained the formalist style of the Fair.

Davis's intention was to create a mural which would look like an enormous blackboard, with white line drawings (each line, due to the scale, would be 3.4 inches wide) on a black ground. His very first notation, dated January 8, stipulates that the mural have the "Quality of a flat surface, decorated by hand." There follow long, well-researched lists of objects, images, and ideas associated with various means of communication (speech, television, postal service etc.), the import of which he summed up in the statement "History of Communication is mechanical objectification of the human Eye, Ear, Voice and Hand." The next day he has worked out his method:

1/9/39
Procedure in Construction of World's Fair Mural
1. Collection of factual visual material
2. Theoretical formulation of function, character, and technique of mural
3. Selection of individual elements, from aesthetic standpoint, which are to be included in the design
4. Aesthetic designing of these elements
5. Inductive composition of these designs to produce new space objects

His procedure determined, he turned to the function of the mural, which he understood in terms of the psychology of advertising which permeated the Fair:

The function of this mural then is concerned only with the aesthetics of the subject. It must convey to the spectator a feeling or a mood which will be remembered by [him] as beautiful or emotionally pleasant and stimulating. In recalling this mural the spectator will not remember dates, costumes, materials of construction, correct historical sequence, or factual information; but he will have a pleasant and stimulating recollection of shape-objects in space in relation to each other.

The value of this kind of expression to the communication industries is that it implants the consciousness of their value on the plane of aesthetics in addition to the other planes of consciousness which have been impressed by more appropriate means.

Davis concluded that the "only thing to work toward is a personally felt design" made up of elements from the objective history of communications. From this point, he proceeds in his notes to record an elaborate rationalization of modernist art, in effect rearticulating the most advanced theorizing of his time on the problem of just what Art is. Reading these brilliant and eloquent pages it is hard not to wonder if the artist ratiocinates not a little too much—if, having stated that his Communications mural has been contrived with all the subliminal craft of a stylish Burma-Shave billboard, he must now drown out his uneasy conscience with some resounding rhetoric.

On January 10 he utters the following incantation:

"Fine Art" means a work which is beautiful and its beauty is the result of the physical order of the elements within the work of Art. This means that a work of Art is complete in itself. It is an end in itself and not a spur to action but to contemplation . . . Therefore I will this mural to be a work of Art made of special elements associated with Communications. I will it to be simple and easy to remember. . .

Volition, of course, precludes spontaneity and all those expressive values which inhere in geomancy; it demands that order prevail.

It is not surprising then to find on January 25 a notation stating "Art is a real topographical order in two dimensions." Davis continues on January 30 to draft a lengthy and brilliant defense of his position. He proposes to give a "precise meaning" to the term "Art," which he always capitalizes. Rejecting Clive Bell's notion of "significant form" as "too vague," he goes on to assert that a

Philip Guston at work on the cartoon for "Maintaining America's Skills." (FVO'C, courtesy Hurlburt)

specific work can have "genuine social value" by conveying a propagandistic message while at the same time failing as a work of Art because it does not convey "an Art experience." On the other hand, an artist indifferent to social issues can create a great work of Art which still manifests social content because "the creation of Art itself is a positive and progressive social value." He posits a clear distinction between "Art content" and "social content" and grants their possible co-existence in the same work. But he argues vigorously against the Marxist idea that a work of art must be understood as a historical unity of form and content, and claims universality only for the formal elements.

For Davis, it is "the profound order of the physical structure" in a work of art and not anything smacking of metaphor or metaphysics that constitutes what he means by Art. He goes on to state that "The appetite which Art satisfies is the hunger for physical stability in the space of the three-dimensional world"—and it is the appeasing of that hunger for survival that constitutes the social role of Art.

> The social content of Art is always simply Art itself. The social meaning of Art consists at all times of an affirmation of the joy felt in the successful resolution of a problem. This expression has social meaning because it gives concrete proof of the possibility of establishing order in certain aspects of man's relation to Nature. Such expression is a moral force and provides courage for life to those who experience it.

The fantasy of art, then, for Davis, is the fantasy of planning. For him the ordering of Nature by selective exclusion becomes the means by which safety within chaos is achieved. Consequently, the artist's own dependence upon, and satisfaction from, this mechanism of defense, becomes the social value of his creative effort. He articulates a fantasy of art as salvific agent first, for the artist, and then, of *his* psychological necessity, for his art's public. To call such an attitude anti-humanist might seem ungenerous. But to believe that an artist's ability to impose order on his design problems—his layout—is a moral act with profound social implications is to impose a naïve and unwarranted projection of his psychological needs upon the body politic. Such an attitude is that of a totalitarianism which views its ambition of order as both moral and inevitable.

As we have seen, such an attitude was not unknown to the industrial designers who contributed to the thinking behind Davis's Communications Building mural, a work he was constrained to "will" to be a moral force. As we shall see, such attitudes were found to be a "usable" aesthetic for the "high" art of the 1960s.

THE USABLE FUTURE ATTAINED: THE FANTASY OF THE NOW

> The presence of two artists like Smith and Pollock, both products of a completed assimilation of French art, relieves us somewhat of the necessity of being apologetic about American art. But they are far from being enough. The art of no country can live and perpetuate itself exclusively on spasmodic feeling, high spirits and the infinite subdivision of sensibility. A substantial art requires balance and enough thought to put it in accord with the most advanced view of the world obtaining at the time. Modern man has *in theory* solved the great public and private questions, and the fact that he has not solved them in practice and that actuality has become more problematical than ever in our day ought not to prevent, in this country, the development of a bland, large, balanced, Apollonian art in which passion does not fill in the gaps left by the faulty or omitted application of theory but takes off from where the most advanced theory stops, and in which an intense detachment informs all. Only such an art, resting on rationality but without permitting itself to be rationalized, can adequately answer contemporary life, found our sensibilities, and, by containing and vicariously relieving them, remunerate us for those particular and necessary frustrations that ensue from living at the present moment in the history of western civilization.

> *Clement Greenberg, "The Present Prospects of American Painting and Sculpture," London: Horizon, October 1947, p. 27.*

The idealist theme of the Fair—"A happier way of American living through the recognition of the interdependence of man and the building of the world of tomorrow"—was somewhat

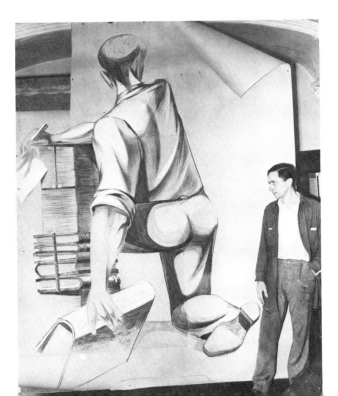

Anton Refregier with his cartoon for a figure in his mural, "Cultural Activities of the WPA," March 1939. (NA)

Stuart Davis and assistant working on the cartoon for "Communications," 1938. (RD)

eclipsed by concurrent events in Europe and Asia. Within a year of its closing, the generation most likely to have been impressed by the spectacle of Flushing Meadow went to war. After 1945 they set about, perhaps the wiser concerning the "interdependence of man," to find their fortune in the "world of tomorrow." In many ways psychological survivors, their future had better be usable. The G.I. Bill gave these men (and some women) an education; a booming postwar economy gave them jobs. By 1950—in their late twenties or early thirties—they were on their way toward creating one of the most thriving consumer societies in history. By 1960 those most capable of enterprise were educated, affluent, and leisured. They constituted (if I may conflate the metaphors of the era) a lonely crowd of proto-robber barons in gray flannel suits seeking status as culture-consuming tastemakers. By 1965 even the Federal government, through its new National Foundations for the Arts and the Humanities, had to acknowledge that tax-supported art patronage was no longer a matter of work-relief for the unemployed, but a politically acceptable method of equalizing the disparity in an economy based on high technology where the arts were still trying to make cottage industries break even.

By the mid-1960s a new patron class numbering about thirty-five to forty million and increasing rapidly [18] found itself with spare cash to spend and a technologically created vacuum to fill. For the most part, this new class turned to the entertainment arts and popular literature; to a lesser extent it turned to the visual arts for status and investment potential. While International Style architecture determined its ideal environment, Pop Art and various modes of geometric abstraction, ranging from Op Art to Color Field and Minimal, found their place on interior walls. A new machine aesthetic was born and bought. [19]

It is curious that a generation for which the 1930s were a dim and depressing memory came to support those two styles of current art which continued the thematic concerns of that decade.

Pop Art's facetious social realism had of course transmuted social commitment into the irony of High Camp. Geometric abstraction, however, became no special taste—but the artistic mode of a decade dominated by a new generation of artists and patrons. The art establishment's metaphors for the era of Kennedy, the New Frontier, Vietnam, racial unrest, Johnson, the Great Society, the counter-culture, and Nixon, were crafted by Andy Warhol and Kenneth Noland rather than Ben Shahn and Stuart Davis. If the "triumph of American painting" occurred during the cold war years of Truman, Korea, the McCarthy witch-hunts, and Eisenhower, it is clear now that even the critics most associated with the rise of Abstract Expressionism felt it wanting and lacking in the "remuneration" of which Greenberg wrote. In short, a decade of unmatched affluence and devastating crisis needed and inevitably got the iconographic defense mechanisms of satire and intellectualized order. High seriousness, when required, could be expressed with a giggle or a theorem—without fear of boring. Only the children of the new leisure class turned to geomancy—and with a vengeance. But neither Happenings (a dimension of Pop Art) nor Psychedelic Art (an envisioning of the drug culture) "made it" in the art world. They were threatening rather than distracting. For money was involved in all this and insurance was needed. Thus evolved the need for certifiable quality.[20]

The idea of quality during the 1960s was used in ways comparable to the streamlining of the 1930s—as a means of rationalizing the modernity of merchandise. But a painting is not a refrigerator, and, though both may have as their only visual virtue a certain "rightness of form," a painting is best invested with an aura of mystery, lest it lose its cool when sold. A label was needed with unimpeachable advertising potential; "quality" was selected, since it had a long history of usage by merchants—comparable only to the seductiveness of the adjective "choice" when affixed to a melon. Therefore quality in art became an unchallengeable moral imperative.

First, it was used as an all-purpose synonym for human reference or expressiveness in a work of art. The effect of this can be sensed but shouldn't be mentioned unless you are going to step outside the limits of criticism and act as "men of letters" or "iconographers."

Second, the word quality was used as beauty and significant form once had been as the veritable last word. You simply had to be sufficiently perspicacious, sensitive, intelligent, and moral to know what *it* meant. The critic is thus free to assert the presence of quality in anything, and those who protest because they do not discern it (because it may not be there) are declared wanton.

Third, the word was construed as an indicator of what was currently being pushed, so the initiates would not make the *faux pas* of walking past the blank canvas or colored cube without proper genuflection. As such, it was often suspiciously interchangeable with the simple concept of fashionable. Quality was, therefore, a cop-out, a put-down, and a code term for what was in.

Such verbal strategies were necessary to compensate for

the visual illiteracy of the new patron class. Though possessing college and graduate degrees, this new audience of apparatchicks had been deprived of liberal educations in the post-sputnik panic for national scientific superiority. Even more serious for the visual arts, their cultural level was fixated at the verbal—their eyes "read" art but could not see it. The visual arts, foreign to their education and personal experience, yet by definition essential to their level of social and economic pretension, required middlemen skilled in words to help them comprehend what they were all too eager to buy and display. Never have sheep been led more eagerly to the fleecing.

Thus the desire to collect and own "quality" modernist art became a serious ambition during the 1960s for more Americans than ever before in the history of the country. While the art of the past—the School of Paris, the Impressionists, even the Old Masters—was not neglected among the more discerning and affluent, the art of the NOW was more fun than the stock market. And the art writers, the various magazines, the museums and the dealers all helped sort through the bewildering array of new work in a swirl of controversy, prestige, and glamour that did indeed "remunerate" the organization man "for those particular and necessary frustrations" of his quotidian existence.[21]

Part of the allure, of course, was the congruency of the art world to the business and industrial world. The new art was modern in its scientism, in its compatibility with cybernetics, in its tendency to appear in new models each year, in its intellectual clarity made apparent by the art writers. Everything about the new art was carefully—sometimes brilliantly—explained by the intellectual descendants of Teague and Bel Geddes. It was clearly recognized at the time that the elaborate rationalizations of the art writers constituted much of the "content" of the art itself. These explanations of "Systemic Painting." "Serial Art," "Primary Structures," and the like [22] quickly became art-historical shibboleths to be referred to in the next round of interpretations. This, of course, permitted the principle of planned obsolescence to be carefully adjusted to the investment requirements of the new patrons and what was transcended in the axiometrically relentless progress of art automatically became art history. What the art writers finished, the curators maintained. The dealers simply suggested from time to time that a collector "complete" his hoard with the very newest or something previously overlooked. Of course, it should be said that this elaborate continuing process required no nefarious conspiracy. It required only the application of sane marketing principles—for the most part invented by the advertising firms and industrial designers of the 1930s—to the world of the visual arts.

The fantasy of the NOW in the art of the 1960s was rooted in a psychologically achieved, rather than an anticipated, future; the "usable future" was NOW. The generation that knew the Depression mostly in terms of its parents' memories and fear, who had been raised for a "better day," had good reason, during the boom years of the 1960s, to feel that the future was theirs. The NOW generation had the pleasure of presuming, on the not inconsiderable evidence of its technology, that it was living the ultimate realization of the modern. The art of its era confirmed that presumption in four ways: perfection of facture, seriality, replicability, and scale.

The purity of form of the Trylon and Perisphere was marred by the crudity of their external facture. Close up, their rough, stuccoed surfaces showed all the signs of hand-, rather than machine-crafting. As Meikle puts it, they looked "as if someone had pasted burlap to wooden forms." [23] As with a heavily-brushed, representational painting, distance was required to lend enchantment. During the 1960s such evidence of hand-facture was banished from art; a certain anonymity of perfection became the ideal. New materials from industrial sources permitted a miraculous impeccability of surface. Just as enameled steel and plastics had permitted the formal rightness of streamlining, acrylics and plexiglas determined the new suavity of line and surface that, coupled with the pure forms of geometry, provided infinite opportunities for decorative permutations.

Seriality permitted formal problems to be worked out systematically and had the added advantage of efficiently emulating the phases of traditional artists. A new series of paintings provided that year's show as well as contrast with the one previous and the one to come. Series of works also permitted patrons to acquire similar but not necessarily identical works. The artist's studio became an assembly line, manufacturing rows of unique objects in the supposed spirit of Monet's haystacks.

Closely related to seriality was the replication of images. "Multiples" became a fad. Editions of small sculptures, posters, and fine prints abounded, revolutionizing the world of prints in general. Because of the enormous sophistication of printing technology, the size of color prints grew to the scale of small easel paintings. These found a vast market among younger and less affluent collectors.

The dramatic increase in the size of prints was paralleled by a dramatic increase in the size of paintings. To discuss these often elephantine works in terms of the traditional concept of scale is difficult, since the relational factors which determine a sense of scale (as opposed to mere dimension)—namely relation to an architectural or environmental setting, or to human height and reach, or to a complex set of internal formal juxtapositions —usually was missing. Instead, size was achieved sheerly for its own sake simply because the technology to achieve it—like that for the SST—was available. Paintings and wall constructions ranging from twenty to nearly a hundred feet in length became common. Yet their mural-like scale was belied by the fact that they hung on walls as would easel paintings; they mostly created environments in the pages of the art magazines. Scale equalled merely bigness as the content of art became that of an inflated problem solving.

Another important development of the 1960s was the increase in corporate involvement in the arts. While the formal developments of the 1960s had roots in the geometric spirit of the Fair more than in the artistic practice of its era, it was certainly the Fair that institutionalized the patronage of the arts by Big Business. The "art" of the industrial designers taught business the utility of aesthetics and as the consumer society of the 1960s became more aesthetically aware, those industries which depended on the buying masses saw art patronage as another form of sound public relations. While most of the available funds have gone to the entertainment arts, a good share has gone to sponsor museum exhibitions and to establish corporate collections. In many instances, corporations have turned to modern architecture to enhance their "image" and have encouraged and supported vast new commercial and cultural centers to improve the "image" of the communities in which they do business.

Indeed, the large-scale realization of the fantasy of the NOW and the final achievement of the usable future—foreshadowed in the attitudes of those who conceived the Fair—is to be found not only in the arts of painting and sculpture but also in the art of monumental architecture as practiced during the 1960s.

Despite the hegemony of the International Style, and its elegant geometries throughout the period which followed the Fair, the vision of the city of tomorrow prevailed when communities and institutions sought to erect public monuments to their sense of modernity.

If one looks carefully at the various model cities at the Fair—and at the Fair itself—certain formal characteristics stand out in sharp contrast to the rectilinearities of the International Style. These can be described as follows: unarticulated plane and curved surfaces, often of vast dimensions; the overpass or urban bridge, separating pedestrians from vehicular traffic; the use of the triangle as an architectural module; the use of battered construction—exemplified by the inclining walls of the Trylon; the apparent challenge to gravity resulting from sophisticated engineering innovations; and the general domination of the site for dramatic effect.

Architectural monuments such as the Charles Center complex in Baltimore, the Renaissance Center in Detroit, the East Building of the National Gallery of Art in Washington, D.C., the Nelson A. Rockefeller Mall in Albany, New York, the Gateway Arch in St. Louis, and New York's Kennedy Airport (to name structures which have conspicuously impressed themselves upon their regions) can all be related to one or more of these formal characteristics.

By far the chief characteristic common to all these monuments is their domination of site, the iconographic implications of their conspicuousness. They stand out as separate and very modern entities in their environments, signs of their cities, historic, cultural and/or economic achievements. In several cases they have come to symbolize the cities they dominate. As such, they are all, in effect, descendents of the Trylon and Perisphere.

In all of these structures the overpass or bridge from one part to the other is a distinguishing element. Indeed, at the Fair, the various overpasses—from the simple structures across the local highways to the floating circular platforms within the Perisphere—constituted exciting and practical architectural innovations, which possessed a high degree of modern ambiance. The pedestrian walkways at the Charles Center, the sweeping ramps at Kennedy, the various staircases and roadways at Rockefeller Mall, the dramatic interior bridges in Washington and Detroit, which culminate in the great Gateway Arch (it must be crossed by all who enter it)—all mark these buildings with an air of radical modernity that has established them as symbolic landmarks.

In many of these structures the triangle takes on an important role in the overall design. It is the module on which the entire Washington complex is constructed. It is also, in a different way, the basis of Gateway Arch. The plans of the Albany buildings are all triangles and major walls are battered. Of all these sites, the Albany Mall most resembles the Fair if only because Wallace Harrison, the architect of the Trylon and Perisphere (and other Fair buildings), designed it. The vast reflecting pools of the mall are lined with buildings that could have been found in either Democracity or the City of Tomorrow. Dominating the vast podium is a Meeting Center in the shape of a huge ovoid that recalls, but does not imitate, the Perisphere. Below, in the concourse, is a collection of the geometric abstraction of the 1960s—indeed, some of the largest canvases of that period. The surrounding gardens are filled with the sculpture of the era.

The single work of monumental American architecture which seems most directly descended from the World of Tomorrow at Flushing Meadow is the St. Louis Gateway Arch. Although it was not erected until between 1959 and 1964, Eero Saarinen won the competition for the Arch in 1948, and thus it was conceived nearer in time to the Fair than the other monuments mentioned.

Saarinen's design is the only major work of architectural sculpture in America that equals the purity of form and the visual drama of the Trylon and Perisphere. Indeed, if one were to take two Trylons, plant their bases 630 feet apart, and bend them into a perfect catenary curve attached at the tops, one would have the simple, three-sided element of the Gateway Arch.

No twentieth-century monument so dominates an American city. Only the great obelisk of the Washington Monument is its equal. But, from every point in St. Louis, Saarinen's "absolutely simple shape"[24] dominates every vista, leaping across the sky to connect older structures with a permanent modern bridge of gleaming metal standing, just as the Trylon and Perisphere stood for a time, as a bridge between the present and a usable future.

We have observed how the Fair, and the art and architecture it contained, was impelled by a fantasy of planning and design as moral redemption, with geometry as the vehicle for moral order in society. Now we have reason to perceive that such faith in geometric thinking is fantastic if not fallacious, especially in light of the contrived and sterile art and architecture of the 1960s. We can also perceive the Fair itself as an exercise in geomantic thinking—but in the service of order, not unity. As such, the Fair promoted psychological manipulation rather than psychological growth. It was thrown down at Flushing Meadow by sophisticated men looking down on carefully ordered maps and models—men who understood the emotional seductiveness of centralized plans, the magic of motorways threading the land, the allure of those cones, cylinders, and spheres geometric thinkers from Socrates to Cezanne had declared the essence of nature. Now *they* declared it the essence of modernism. If visitors to the Fair could not readily perceive the unity implied by the Fair itself, because of its overweening scale, they could sense the order, the centrality, the controlling purposiveness designed into it to show the way to the future. Just as the fascist leaders of Europe had marshalled archetypes to their tyrannical causes, the industrial designers innocently sought to sell goods with their fantasy of a consumer society. The Fair was planned to keep people greedy rather than to prompt generosity; it was a place where an order was imposed by those who felt they knew best, at the expense of a more comprehensive economic, social, and environmental unity. The geomantic potential of art was corrupted and applied to that end. It became only another commodity to be consumed in the usable future. The history of the last forty years suggests that the Fair succeeded all too well in symbolizing the fantasies of its creators—and in determining those of its children.

NOTES

1. Alfred Haworth Jones, "The Search for a Usable American Past in the New Deal Era," *American Quarterly*, XXIII (December 1971): 710-724; and Jeffrey L. Meikle, *Twentieth Century Limited: Industrial Design in America, 1925-1939* (Philadelphia: Temple University Press, 1979)—hereafter Meikle.

2. See, for instance, Erik H. Erikson, *Insight and Responsibility* (New York: W.W. Norton & Co., 1964), pp. 120-122; James Hillman, *Re-Visioning Psychology* (New York: Harper and Row, 1975), pp. 38-42; Peter Gay, *Art and Act: On Causes in History—Manet, Gropius, Mondrian* (New York: Harper and Row, 1976), p. 19.

3. "The New York World's Fair," *Legion d'Honneur*, IX (July 1938), p. 14, quoted by Joan M. Marter, "Modern American Sculpture at the New York World's Fair, 1939" in *Vanguard American Sculpture: 1913-1939* (New Brunswick: Rutgers University Art Gallery, 1979), pp. 140-149. The Trylon and Perisphere is called a "primary structure" here for the first time and seen as a prototype for such works in the 1960s. Unfortunately the description of the theme center is not precise.

4. I have drawn on the ideas expressed in Walter Dorwin Teague, *Design This Day: The Technique of Order in the Machine Age* (New York: Harcourt Brace, 1940); and two books by Norman Bel Geddes: *Horizons* (Boston: Little Brown, 1932) and *Magic Motorways* (New York: Random House, 1940).

5. Teague, *Design This Day*, op. cit.

6. Meikle, pp. 176-7.

7. For the Platonic ideal of planned obsolescence, see Meikle, pp. 93-5.

8. Philip J. Pauly, "Psychology at Hopkins," *Johns Hopkins Magazine* (December, 1979), p. 40; and Meikle, pp. 71-2.

9. Henry Dreyfuss, "Scheme for the Theme Exhibit: A resume of what will take place in the Perisphere at the New York World's Fair 1939," manuscript presentation portfolio dated 12/13/38, Dreyfuss Archive 72.88.159, Cooper-Hewitt Museum of Design, Smithsonian Institution, New York; "The Theme Center—Democracity," *Official Guide Book of the New York World's Fair 1939* and sub. eds.; Meikle, Chapter Nine passim.

10. For general information and critical assessments of the art at the Fair, see: *Magazine of Art*, 32 (May 1939) passim; *The Art Digest*, XIII (June 1, 1939) passim;

Parnassus X (December 1938), pp. 6-9; *The New York Times*, "World's Fair Section," (March 5, 1939) passim; and *The New York Herald Tribune*, "World's Fair Section," (April 30, 1939) passim. All contain reproductions of the murals and sculpture at the Fair, the last two sometimes in color.

11. See Olive Lyford Gavert, "The WPA Federal Art Project and the New York World's Fair, 1939-1940," in Francis V. O'Connor, editor, *The New Deal Art Projects: An Anthology of Memoirs* (Washington, D.C.: Smithsonian Institution Press, 1972), pp. 247-267. See *American Art Today*, introduction by Holger Cahill (New York: National Art Society, 1939) for reproductions of all the works in the exhibit. The 1940 exhibit changed periodically and did not have a formal catalogue. For Cahill's philosophy of art and society, and his interest in John Dewey, see his foreword to Francis V. O'Connor, editor, *Art for the Millions: Essays from the 1930s by Artists and Administrators of the WPA Federal Art Project* (Greenwich, Connecticut: New York Graphic Society, 1973), pp. 33-44.

12. From a WPA Art Program planning document dated 1940. National Archives Record Group 69, Regional and State Correspondence, New York City, Box 42. Other boxes which contain WPA material relating to the Fair are 57, 75, 2055-58, 2108-9.

13. *The Art Digest*, op. cit., pp. 15 and 36-38.

14. *Parnassus*, op. cit., p. 8.

15. From a manuscript in the files of the author.

16. See E. C. Goosen, *Stuart Davis*, The Great American Artists Series (New York: George Braziller, 1959); Diane Kelder, editor, *Stuart Davis*, Documentary Monographs in Modern Art (New York: Praeger Publishers, 1971); Zabriskie Gallery, New York. *Stuart Davis: Murals—An Exhibition of Related Studies*, introduction by Beth Urdang, January 27—February 14, 1976; John R. Lane, *Stuart Davis: Art and Art Theory* (The Brooklyn Museum, 1979), Chapter 3.

17. Kelder, *Stuart Davis*, op. cit., p. 17.

18. Alvin Toffler, *The Culture Consumers: A Study of Art and Affluence in America* (New York: St. Martin's Press, 1964), p. 22.

19. For a wide range of the art criticism of the 1960s, see Gregory Battcock, editor, *The New Art: A Critical Anthology* and *Minimal Art: A Critical Anthology* (New York: E.P. Dutton, 1966 and 1968 respectively).

20. See Michael Kirby, *Happenings: An Illustrated Anthology* (E.P. Dutton, 1965) and Robert E.L. Masters and Jean Houston, *Psychedelic Art* (New York: Grove Press, 1968).

21. Francis V. O'Connor, "Notes on Patronage: The 1960s," *Artforum* (September 1972), pp. 52-56.

22. See Battcock, *Minimal Art*, op. cit., passim, for these and similar titles.

23. Meikle, p. 190. Harrison originally wanted the surface stuccoed to a perfect finish, but that was not economically feasible.

24. Aline B. Saarinen, editor, *Eero Saarinen on His Work* (New Haven: Yale University Press, 1968), p. 22.

Francis V. O'Connor is a free-lance historian of twentieth-century American art specializing in the period from 1930 to the present. The author of five books, he is currently writing a history of the American mural.

CATALOGUE OF THE EXHIBITION

The exhibition is arranged thematically, in a fashion similar to the Fair itself. Material is catalogued according to function—communications, transportation, amusement—or relationship to the theme—government, community interests, medicine, public health—of the respective zones. An effort has been made to place exhibits within their actual zones at the Fair; where this has proved impractical, discrepancies are explained in the annotations.

Only primary objects appear in this catalogue. The exhibits are supplemented with uncatalogued photographs, documents, and memorabilia, for which a separate checklist is available. However, lenders of both catalogued and uncatalogued material are listed at the back of this volume.

Measurements of artworks are in inches, with height preceding width. Three-dimensional objects, including sculpture, architectural models, and mechanical devices, are measured by height, width, and depth unless otherwise noted.

Billy Rose's "Aquabelles" admire Tony Sarg's cartoon map of the Fair (cat. no. 126).

BACKGROUND

Robert Moses (left), Grover Whalen (center) and Fiorello La Guardia examine plans for Fair access roads, while Fair construction proceeds in the background. (PMW)

WESTINGHOUSE ELECTRIC CORPORATION

1. TIME CAPSULE. (replica), 1938.
   Cupaloy (copper, chrome and silver alloy) casing, length 96; diameter 8.
   Lent by Westinghouse Corporation.

The TIME CAPSULE was assembled and deposited by the Westinghouse Electric Corporation as part of its Fair exhibit. The sealing-in ceremonies took place at noon on September 23, 1938. The contents of the Capsule fall into five groupings:

I. SMALL ARTICLES OF COMMON USE that we wear or use, or which contribute to our comfort, convenience, safety, or health.

II. TEXTILES AND MATERIALS. About seventy-five in number, these comprise swatches of various types and weaves of cloth, samples of alloys, plastics, cement, asbestos, coal, etc.

III. MISCELLANEOUS ITEMS. Seeds, books, money, type, special texts, etc.

IV. AN ESSAY IN MICROFILM, comprising books, speeches, excerpts from books and encyclopedias, pictures, critiques, reports, circulars, timetables, and other printed or

written matter, the whole producing in logical order a description of our time, our arts, sciences, techniques, sources of information, and industries. The essay, divided into fifteen sub-sections, contains the equivalent of more than 100 ordinary books, a total of more than 22,000 pages, more than 10,000,000 words and 1,000 pictures.

V. NEWSREEL. Characteristic or significant scenes in sound film prepared by RKO-Pathe Pictures, Inc. for the Time Capsule. Instructions for making a suitable projection machine for this film are included in the microfilm Micro-File.

Among the indicative items are: a Mickey Mouse child's cup; a Woolworth rhinestone clip; "The Story of Rockefeller Center"; reproductions of paintings by Picasso, Mondrian, Dali, and Grant Wood; the sheet music of "Flat Foot Floogie"; Gone With the Wind; photographs of a radio broadcast; the Daily Worker for August 30, 1938 (along with eight other New York dailies); the Sears, Roebuck catalogue for 1938-39. The newsreel included film of: the veterans' reunion on the 75th anniversary of the Battle of Gettysburg; Howard Hughes's July 1938 record-breaking

round-the-world flight in his Lockheed 14, called "New York World's Fair 1939"; Jesse Owens winning the 100-meter dash at the 1936 Berlin Olympics; football and baseball games; military displays; the bombing of Canton by Japan (June 1938); a fashion show; and the World's Fair Preview Motorcade of April 30, 1938.

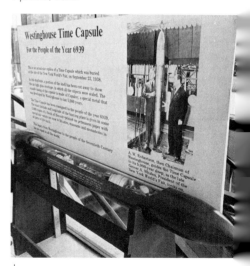

1.

74

GORDON W. GILKEY

2. NEW YORK WORLD'S FAIR SITE,
FLUSHING BAY, undated (1938).
Etching, 6⅜ x 8⅞ (image), signed in pencil.
Lent by the Library of Congress.

*This and the other exhibited etchings by Gilkey
are from a suite of fifty-four prints
commissioned by the World's Fair Corporation
and published in a facsimile edition by Charles
Scribner's Sons in 1939.*

H. M. PETTIT

3. Aerial view of New York World's Fair of
1939, undated (ca. 1938).
Tempera on wallboard, 43¼ x 84½.
Lent by the Portledge School, Locust
Valley, N.Y.

*"How the New York World's Fair will look at
its gala opening next April 30 is depicted in
this official painting by H. M. Pettit.
Tree-shaded avenues radiate in rainbow colors
from the white Perisphere and Trylon (ball and
spire), theme symbol of the Fair. In the
background (upper section of painting), rise the
towers of New York City. Shapes of buildings
are accurate, with roads and bridges in
perspective." (Released by Associated Press,
January 7, 1939.)*

MILTON M. DUKE

4. Model of Fairgrounds, undated (1937).
Cardboard, paper, catalin plastic and
miscellaneous materials. Length 37¼;
width 16¼.
Lent by Milton M. Duke.

*In 1937 the World's Fair Corporation had its
offices in the Empire State Building, where a
model of the proposed Fair plan was exhibited.
Milton Duke, then fourteen and a keen
amateur model maker, saw the exhibit and
requested a copy of the plan from which to
make his own model. Working from a 6' x 12'
engineer's drawing of the Fairgrounds, Duke
used tweezers and a razor blade to fashion bits
of cardboard, wood, and sponge rubber into
miniature buildings, trees, and vehicles. The
model was exhibited in Pennsylvania Station,
the Broadway branch of Woolworth's, and at
several other locations in the New York-New
Jersey area. The Brooklyn Daily Eagle
reported that Duke spent three and a half
months on the model and that "Milton hopes to
be a civil engineer some day and is getting an*

3.

*early start." (January 8, 1938). Duke did indeed
become an architect and is now Assistant
Commissioner of the Division of Housing and
Community Renewal of the State of New York.*

BOARD OF DESIGN

5. NEW YORK WORLD'S FAIR 1940 LOT
RENTING PLAN, SECTION 1.
Ink on linen, 38 x 24.
Lent by the Department of Parks, City of
New York.

DEPARTMENT OF PARKS

6. GENERAL DEVELOPMENT PLAN,
FLUSHING MEADOW PARK, February
1936.
Photostat on paper, 24 x 55½.
The Queens Museum, gift of Frank
Pokorney.

*In January 1938, Robert Moses, Park
Commissioner of the City of New York, wrote
in the Saturday Evening Post of his scheme
for the reclamation of Flushing Meadow.
Beginning in 1932 with the construction of the
Grand Central Parkway, Moses's plan involved
the complete re-engineering of the site, and
the proposed Fair gave him the opportunity to
secure funds for the project.*

NEMBHARD N. CULIN

7. Six caricature sketches of Fair executives,
undated (ca. 1936).
Pencil on paper, each 10 x 7⅞.

WHALEN (Grover A. Whalen, President
of the Fair Corporation).

Milton Duke with his model of the Fair
(cat. no. 4). (Duke)

MR. KOHN (Robert D. Kohn, Chairman,
Committee on Theme).

COM. FLANIGAN (Howard A. Flanigan,
Vice President and Administrative
Assistant to the President).

COL. HOGAN (John P. Hogan, Vice
President and Chief Engineer).

VOORHEES (Stephen F. Voorhees, Vice
President and Chief Architect; Chairman,
Board of Design).

ANDREWS (W. Earle Andrews, General
Engineering Consultant).

Lent by the artist.

7. WHALEN

7. ANDREWS

7. VOORHEES

9.

LUCILLE CORCOS

8. 1939 WORLD'S FAIR, undated (ca. 1939).
Tempera on masonite, 17½ x 13½.
Signed, lower left: Corcos.
Lent by Beverly and Ray Sacks,
Cedarhurst, N. Y.

JAMES THURBER

9. Cover drawing for *The New Yorker,* April
29, 1939.

Ink on illustration board, with overlay of
watercolor on tracing paper, 14 x 10¼
(image).
Signed, lower right: James Thurber.
Lent by the Museum of the City of New
York.

PAUL HOWARD MANSHIP

10. TIME AND THE FATES OF MAN, 1938.
(Scale model of sundial, Constitution
Mall).
Bronze, 52½ x 62¾ x 9.
Signed and dated, top of base, left: Paul
Manship © 1938.
Lent by the National Collection of Fine
Arts, Smithsonian Institution, gift of Paul
Manship.

11. THE MOODS OF TIME, 1938. (Scale
models of fountain figures, Constitution
Mall.)

MORNING
Bronze. Height, 14; length, 22¾.
Signed and dated on cloud:
Paul Manship © 1938.

DAY
Bronze. Height, 13½; length, 26¼.
Signed and dated on cloud:
Paul Manship © 1938.

EVENING
Bronze. Height, 13½; length, 21.
Signed and dated on cloud:
Paul Manship © 1938.

NIGHT
Bronze. Height, 15½; length, 25½.
Signed and dated on cloud:
Paul Manship © 1938.
Lent by the National Collection of Fine
Arts, Smithsonian Institution, gift of
Paul Manship

*The sundial, with its four pendant Moods of
Time, was located in the central mall, between
the Theme Center and the monumental statue
of George Washington, by James Earle Fraser,
that stood in Washington Square. The dial's
eighty-foot gnomon rested on a bending Tree
of Life, in the shade of which the Three Fates—
Past, Present, and Future—bound together by
the Thread of Life, were shown working out
Man's destiny.*

12.

Full-size version, "Time and the Fates of Man," destroyed. (PMW)

8.

MORGAN, HAMEL AND ENGELKEN, engineers

12. AQUALONS FOR PLAZA VI NORTH, 1938.
   Pencil on tracing paper, 30 x 42⅛.
   Dated, lower right, February 27, 1938.
   Lent by the Department of Parks, City of New York.

   "AQUALONS These glass cylinders combine an architectural form with water, light and color to produce a decorative effect. Bubbles of air and the circulation of water amusingly animate the peace and harmony of the Courts."
   (Information Manual, February 28, 1939)

ARTIST UNKNOWN

13. Sketch for proposed placement of monumental statue of George Washington by James Earle Fraser, undated (ca. 1936).
   Pencil on tracing paper, 12¼ x 15.
   Lent by Herbert Starkman.

11. DAY

The Theme Center at sunset.

14. NEW YORK WORLD'S FAIR 1939
(prospectus of proposed international
exposition), (New York: New York
World's Fair 1939, Inc., 1936).
Bound in leatherette, 24⅜ x 18¾.
Lent by Sandra Sperber.

HUGH FERRISS, delineator

15. Rendering of proposed Theme Center
(unexecuted), 1936.
Charcoal and white chalk on illustration
board, 29½ x 25⅞.
Signed and dated, lower right: Hugh
Ferriss 1936; inscribed, lower right: Board
of Design 9/ Sept. 1, 1936.
Lent by the Museum of the City of New
York.

*Hugh Ferriss, an architect and renderer whose
visionary book, Metropolis of Tomorrow,
was published in 1929, was one of the Board of
Design's four official delineators, responsible
for rendering concepts of general plans and
theoretical structures for promotional
purposes. His drawing for a Theme Center with
round auditorium and two monumental towers
was reproduced in the Theme Edition of the*

*World's Fair Bulletin (November 1936) as
"Design of Theme Building and Tower,...
dominating the whole like the lofty cathedral of
a medieval town,...projected to rise in simple
dignity 250 feet above the core of the Fair."*

*On November 24, 1936, Grover Whalen
signed a contract with Wallace K. Harrison and
J. André Fouilhoux for a commission to design a
Theme Center for the Fair. The New York
Times reported that "although sketches have
been made public of a vast circular building
dominated by twin towers, these were entirely
tentative and the design of the building will be
left almost entirely to the discretion of Mr.
Harrison and Mr. Fouilhoux....The architects
were nominated by the board of design and
approved by the board of directors of the fair."*

**HARRISON AND FOUILHOUX,
architects**

16. Preliminary sketch for Theme Center
(unexecuted), undated (ca. 1937).
Charcoal on newsprint, 16 x 24.
Lent by Kevin and Brenda Hom.

HUGH FERRISS, delineator

17. Rendering of Theme Center on imaginary

"pageant night," undated (1937).
Charcoal with white and colored chalk on
illustration board, 20 x 26¼.
Signed, lower left: Hugh Ferriss.
Lent by the Museum of the City of New
York.

18. Rendering of Theme Center on imaginary
"pageant night," 1937.
Charcoal and watercolor on illustration
board, 19⅜ x 26⅛.
Signed and dated, lower left: Hugh Ferriss
'37.
Lent by the Museum of the City of New
York.

15.

Cat. no. 18 was reproduced in Pencil Points, April 1937 (p. 20), with the following statement:

> Mr. Harrison said that in planning the Fair's Theme Center the idea of using some spherical structure came up almost at the beginning....
>
> "We considered a tower fifteen-hundred-feet high; we thought of building a cluster of bowls for open air exhibits; we proposed a great [armillary] sphere which would show the movement of the planets; we conceived

16.

of towers on top of balls and balls on top of towers.

> "Other ideas included a large, glass tower with a spiral track running up to the top, a hoop on top of a sphere with a car swooping around the hoop, various forms of theatres, great rising platforms, twin towers joined at the top, and even a great eagle holding a sphere on its back."

18.

HARRISON AND FOUILHOUX, architects

19. Elevation of Theme Center, undated (ca. 1937).
Photostat on paper, 18⅛ x 24¼.
Stamped, lower left: Harrison and Fouilhoux.
Lent by Kevin and Brenda Hom.

WADDELL AND HARDESTY, consulting engineers

20. TRYLON STRESS SHEET, 1937.
Ink on linen, 30⅜ x 43¾.
Drawn by S.L., dated August 20, 1937.
On extended loan from Hardesty and Hanover, Consulting Engineers.

21. PERISPHERE, UPPER HEMISPHERE, 1937.
Ink on linen, 30⅜ x 43¾.
Drawn by A.E.M., dated August 13, 1937.
On extended loan from Hardesty and Hanover, Consulting Engineers.

Mr. Alfred Hedefine, an engineer of Waddell and Hardesty, recalls that "the Trylon was unique in that it involved the use of a triangular braced tower so slender that the design was controlled by the wind forces rather than the dead and live loads." Owing to the lack of precedents, wind-tunnel tests were conducted. The design shown in the exhibited plans, based on the resulting calculations, involved the reduction of the Trylon's height from the proposed 700 feet to 610 feet, with six-foot tall footings in concrete and a beacon tower of 4' 6", bringing the total height from the ground to 620' 6". The diameter of the Perisphere was reduced from the proposed 200 feet to

180 feet. According to an interview published in 1978, "Mr. Hedefine was able to report that when an observer stood with one foot on the completed Perisphere and the other on the bridge connecting the Perisphere to the Trylon, only the faintest tremor could be detected during a 45-mile wind."

The elevation shown (cat. no. 19) pictures the Theme Center design before the modifications were made; it also illustrates a second helical ramp, running directly from the Perisphere to the ground. In the final design, one ramp served both buildings.

In an interview on April 26, 1979 Harrison discussed the technical difficulties encountered in preparing the design:

> I wanted the architectural contrast of a round dome and a tower. The main problem was how big to make the dome. The only thing we could find that was anything like it was gas storage tanks. We went around the country looking at gas storage tanks, just to get a feeling of how big you make it to make it impressive. We finally decided on about 200 feet as our goal. In the end they took 15% off the size of it and that 15% showed. The ball was always, to me, a little bit too small. The Trylon we were able to get almost to the height we wanted, but they cut that down too. I think the Trylon could have been slightly taller.

Harrison also remarked on his dissatisfaction with the exterior finish of the Theme Center, which was covered in gypsum board coated with tymstone and did not achieve the pristine smoothness the architects had envisioned. "In many ways, it was more beautiful when it was just steel," he said.

The Theme Center under construction, April 1938. (FC)

Views of the Theme Center

Cross-country goodwill motorcade ready
to leave from the Fairgrounds, May 2, 1938.
(PMW)

"Builders of the Future," a sculpture by
William Zorach, in front of the
scaffold-covered Theme Center. (FC)

24.

THEME CENTER — NEW YORK WORLD'S FAIR — 1939

FRANK CRONICAN

22. Model of Theme Center
    Mixed media, 8 x 8½ x 8½.
    Lent by Frank Cronican.

    Frank Cronican was born in Chicago and became interested in fairs after attending the "Century of Progress" exposition. In 1939, he created a model of the New York World's Fair, complete with illumination, in his back yard, attracting the attention of neighbors, passers-by and the press. Upon learning of his achievement, Grover Whalen presented him with an official World's Fair flag (cat. no. 137).

DESIGNER UNKNOWN

23. Official design, 1939 New York World's Fair, 1938.
    Pencil and tempera on paper, mounted on illustration board, 20¼ x 14⅞ (over-all).
    Inscribed, lower left: Approved by Executive Committee April 4, 1938.
    Lent by the Museum of the City of New York.

MAKER UNKNOWN

24. Model of Theme Center, undated (1938).
    Aluminum and steel. Height, 36; diameter of base, 30.
    Inscribed on base: Theme Center — New York World's Fair 1939.
    Lent by The Franklin D. Roosevelt Library, Hyde Park, N.Y.

    This is one of forty-nine models presented to the President and Governors of the states as a goodwill gesture. The models were mounted on the roofs of a fleet of limousines and paraded prior to presentation on May 2, 1938.

GORDON W. GILKEY

25. CONSTRUCTION OF THE THEME BUILDINGS, undated (1938).
    Etching, 8¾ x 6⅞ (image).
    Monogrammed in plate; signed in pencil.
    Lent by the Library of Congress.

26. THE THEME CENTER, undated (1938).
    Etching, soft ground and aquatint, 8⅞ x 6¼ (image).
    Signed in pencil.
    Lent by the Library of Congress.

Theme Center from the Court of Peace, showing night illumination. (AS)

81

COMMUNICATIONS

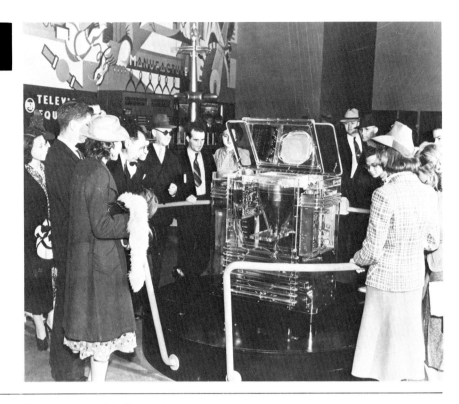

Visitors crowd around the "Transparent Television" in the lobby of the RCA Building. (RCA)

FRANK CRONICAN

27. Model of Communications Building.
(Francis Keally and Leonard Dean, architects)
Mixed media, in plexiglas case,
3¾ x 7¼ x 9¼.
Lent by Frank Cronican.

DONALD DESKEY, designer

28. Rendering of focal exhibit, Hall of Communications, undated (1938).
Watercolor and airbrush on illustration board, 18¾ x 16-3/16.
Lent by the Donald Deskey Archive, Cooper-Hewitt Museum: Smithsonian Institution, New York.

STUART DAVIS

29. HISTORY OF COMMUNICATIONS, 1939. (Sketch for mural, Hall of Communications.)
Ink on paper, 9⅝ x 29⅞.
Signed and dated, lower right: Stuart Davis 1939.
Lent by Mrs. Stuart Davis, courtesy of Grace Borgenicht Gallery, New York.

The focal exhibit of the Communications zone occupied a room 180' x 50' in size and dealt with the effects of modern communications methods on civilization, and the socializing and humanizing force of the dissemination of knowledge. In 1940, owing to the failure to attract a sufficient number of commercial exhibitors to lease the remaining space, the building was amalgamated with Marine Transport and was partially devoted to the displays of nautical exhibitors.

Davis's mural occupied the left-hand wall of the focal exhibit in the Hall of Communications. The work was intended for execution in fluorescent paint, to produce a glowing effect in the semidarkened hall; but, according to the artist's widow, budgetary restrictions were imposed and the work was done in plain white paint on a black background. This mural, along with almost all the other artworks commissioned by the Fair Corporation and the private exhibitors, was destroyed when the Fair was demolished in 1940-1941.

GORDON W. GILKEY

30. RADIO CORPORATION OF AMERICA BUILDING, undated (1938).
Etching, 7⅛ x 8⅞ (image).
Signed in pencil.
Lent by the Library of Congress.

31.

29.

RADIO CORPORATION OF AMERICA

31. Television, console model TRK-12, 1940.
Veneered wood, 39¾ x 34¼ x 18¾.
Lent by Ralph Russo.

On April 20, 1939 David Sarnoff, President of the Radio Corporation of America, dedicated his company's pavilion at the Fair; this was the first news event ever covered by television in the United States. Ten days later, at the Fair's opening ceremonies, Franklin D. Roosevelt became the first American president to make a televised speech. As RCA publicity announced, "now television starts on its way as an important factor in the nation's economic structure."

The transmission of televised pictures had been in the experimental phase for some thirty years prior to the Fair. Various mechanical systems had produced images of poor resolution, and kits, similar to the do-it-yourself radio sets, were available for hobbyists during the 1920s and 1930s. In 1928 RCA established an experimental station, W2XBS, in Schenectady, New York, where pictures were transmitted by the Alexanderson rotating-disc method. With the perfection of the cathode ray tube in the mid 30's, television entered its electronic phase, and in November 1936, after several months of intermittent broadcasts, the British Broadcasting Corporation began transmission of regular programming, using both the mechanical and electronic systems.

RCA reportedly spent $2 million in three years of practical field tests before marketing three receivers in 1939. The radio-TV console TRK-12, retailing for $600, has a 7⅜" x 9¾"

picture viewed by reflection in a mirror set in the cabinet lid. Signals were relayed by the NBC-RCA antenna on the Empire State Building and were estimated to have a reception range of fifty miles. Mobile camera units covered news events at the Fair and made remote broadcasts from various locations on the grounds. Receivers were also shown in the General Electric and Westinghouse buildings. In 1940 DuMont televisions were included in the Crosley exhibit. Also, an experimental television-telephone booth was featured in the Drug Store of Tomorrow in the Hall of Pharmacy.

THOMAS LO MEDICO

32. FAMILY GROUP, undated (1938).
Plaster with golden patina, 24 x 24 x 12.
Lent by the artist.

This piece is the maquette (working model) for a ten-foot sculpture in the display of the Metropolitan Life Insurance Company, in the Business Systems and Insurance Building (Communications and Business Systems zone). The Metropolitan Life display, like the Fair itself, was concerned with reaching the "typical American" in order to communicate a message — in this case, the "security programs" available to the typical American family.

In the final version of the sculpture, the facial features were softened and collars and other details were added to the figures' clothing in an effort to Americanize the group, which was considered Russian-looking by officials of the insurance company.

Detail of Communications mural during execution, seen through scaffolding. (RD)

BELL TELEPHONE LABORATORIES

33. VODER (Voice Operation Demonstrator) synthetic speaker, developed between 1936-1939.
Console 39 (max.) x 35 x 24; speaker unit height: 69, width 20.
Lent by New York Telephone Company.

The VODER was developed especially for the New York and San Francisco fairs from a speech synthesizer demonstrated by Homer W. Dudley of Bell Laboratories at the Harvard Tercentenary in 1936. The machine produced two types of speech sounds — the breathy or hissing sounds and the vibrating (vocal chord) tones — divided into parts by keys "played" by a specially trained operator. Inflection was produced by means of a foot pedal. With the exception of the keys, the VODER's parts were standard telephone equipment.

THE VODER

LYONEL FEININGER

34. Study for courtyard mural, Masterpieces of Art Building, undated (ca. 1939). Watercolor and ink on paper, 9¼ x 50. Signed, lower left: Feininger. Lent by Marlborough Fine Art (London) Ltd.

The Masterpieces of Art Building (Harrison and Fouilhoux, architects) was financed by a consortium of "public-spirited citizens" called Art Associates, Inc., the main backer of which was the Solomon R. Guggenheim Foundation. The exhibition, organized and selected by Dr. William R. Valentiner, Director of the Detroit Institute of Arts, consisted of over 400 paintings from museums and private collections in the U.S. and abroad, surveying European art from the thirteenth through nineteenth centuries. In 1940 the exhibition was expanded to include eighteenth- and nineteenth-century American paintings. At the close of the Fair, the war in Europe made the return of many of the works impractical. Foreign loans were placed in the custodial care of American museums for the duration of the war.

Baroness Hilla Rebay, Director of Guggenheim's Museum of Non-Objective Art, was reponsible for securing the commission for Feininger to decorate the three walls of the building's inner courtyard. In a letter to Alfred Neumeyer (April 3, 1939), Feininger wrote:

...the mural affair has finally materialized. I have the most distinguished commission to decorate the beautiful courtyard of the building Exhibition of Old Masterpieces. That is a still more satisfying task than to organize the design of the outside walls. [Feininger also made sketches for an unexecuted mural on the facade.] I have already submitted my first sketches to the greatest satisfaction of the committee

(financiers, collectors, Director Valentiner, and others), which accepted them. The Courtyard demands three murals; two at a length of 100' each, one of 46'; and they stand at three sides of a pool, which fills the floor and leaves only a path of 10' "dry" for the visitors. Thus results a magic reflection and I calculate the height of the walls at ca. 18'. (Courtesy of the Archives of American Art.)

The exhibited sketch is for the mural on the building's east wall and contains many elements familiar in Feininger's work, including ships (see his sketches for the Marine Transportation Building, cat. nos. 96-98) and a village with arcades, houses, and distant landscapes of barren hills. The Cubistic superimposition of imagery and the use of subtly blended color and dynamic line are characteristic of Feininger's mature style.

The instrument was first demonstrated at the Franklin Institute in Philadelphia in January 1939. Twenty-four Voderettes—switchboard operators from New York Telephone Company—were trained by S. A. Watkins of Bell Labs for nearly a year prior to the fairs. By the second season, some of the Voderettes had become so accomplished that they could make the machine sing, so music was made a feature of the 1940 demonstrations.

The New York Sun reported that, although the VODER could produce a convincing imitation of human speech, it spoke with a "slight electrical accent." Its major stumbling blocks were the transitional sounds of L and R. "'Bell' it could hardly say. That is its most difficult word, on account of the liquid 'l' sound. It couldn't say 'darn'; 'dahn' was its best effort," the Sun observed.

Courtyard, Masterpieces of Art Building, showing east wall at right. (TLF)

Bell Telephone's Voder exhibit, American Telephone and Telegraph Building. (NY Tel. Co.)

34.

A group of visitors poses for a photograph in front of "The Harp," by Augusta Savage. (PMW)

NEMBHARD N. CULIN, designer

35. Rendering of south elevation, Hall of Special Events (Textile Building; Hall of Fashion), undated (ca. 1938). (Frost, Frost & Fenner, architects). Pencil, watercolor, and airbrush on illustration board, 22½ x 32. Lent by the Museum of the City of New York.

Nembhard Culin, a staff member of the Board of Design and a graduate of M.I.T., was responsible for the design of this building and its decorative "hairpin" pylons, as well as many incidental Fair structures, such as information booths, concession stands, street lights, and lighting pylons. Described in the first edition of the Official Guide Book *as the Hall of Fashion, the building was actually used for special events and in 1940 became an operations building. Fashion shows and textile displays were housed in the Consumers Building, which became the World of Fashion in the second season.*

35.

DEPARTMENT OF EXHIBITS (Ian Woodner-Silverman, designer?)

36. COSMETICS (design for proposed exhibit, Hall of Fashion), 1938.
Watercolor and airbrush on illustration board, 20 x 30.
Dated, lower right: Feb. 14, 1938.
Lent by the Museum of the City of New York.

37. RAYON AND SILK (design for proposed exhibit, Hall of Fashion), 1938.
Watercolor, airbrush, and collage on illustration board, 20 x 30.
Dated, lower left: Feb. 14, 1938.
Lent by the Museum of the City of New York.

38. HOSIERY (design for proposed exhibit, Hall of Fashion), 1938.
Watercolor, airbrush, and collage on illustration board, 20 x 29½.
Dated, lower right: Feb. 16, 1938.
Lent by the Museum of the City of New York.

WAYLANDE GREGORY

39. FOUNTAIN OF THE ATOM, six studies for figures, undated (ca. 1938).
Ceramic with partial glaze in polychrome.
Air and *Fire*, height 3.
Four electrons, height 2.
Lent by Nembhard N. Culin.

The Fountain of the Atom, located in Bowling Green at the IRT-BMT entrance to the Community Interests zone, was a thirty-foot glass structure designed by Nembhard Culin. The ceramic sculptures by Waylande Gregory represented the four elements—Earth, Air, Fire, and Water—on the upper tier and on the lower level eight playful "electrons." At night the fountain was illuminated from within and a gas flame rose from the top. The full-size ceramic figures are reported to be in the collection of the artist's widow.

BETTY EPSTEIN

40. Design for figure of a singer for Variety Show, WPA Puppet Theatre, undated (ca. 1938).
Pencil and watercolor on paper, 11¾ x 9.
Signed, lower right: Betty Epstein.
Lent by the Research Center for the Federal Theatre Project, George Mason University, Fairfax, Virginia.

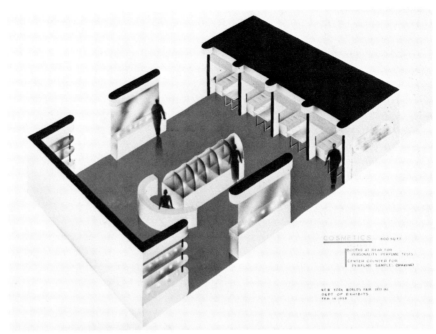

36.

41. Design for figure of a ballet dancer for Variety Show, WPA Puppet Theatre, undated (ca. 1938).
Pencil and watercolor on paper, 11¾ x 9.
Signed, lower right: Betty Epstein.
Lent by the Research Center for the Federal Theatre Project, George Mason University, Fairfax, Virginia.

The WPA Federal Theatre Project staged performances and marionette shows in the WPA Building until June 1939, when it was officially liquidated after a Congressional investigation charged subversive influence within the arts projects. The Theatre Project's productions at the Fair were "Prologue to Glory," a dramatization of Abraham Lincoln's courtship of Ann Rutledge, and two puppet shows, "The Story of Ferdinand" and "String Fever." The two sketches on exhibition are for characters in this latter production.

PHILIP GUSTON

42. Sketch for figure of builder, MAINTAINING AMERICA'S SKILLS (mural on entrance facade, WPA Building), 1939.
Pencil on paper, 14 x 11.
Signed and dated, lower right: Philip Guston, 1939.
Lent by Clifford Ross, courtesy of Salander-O'Reilly Galleries, New York.

43. Sketch for figures, MAINTAINING AMERICA'S SKILLS, undated (ca. 1938).
Pencil on paper, 18 x 24 (sight).
Lent by Mr. and Mrs. Michael Rubinstein, courtesy of Salander-O'Reilly Galleries, New York.

ANTON REFREGIER

44. Color perspective study for two of eight panels, THE CULTURAL ACTIVITIES OF THE WPA (murals for theatre lobby, WPA Building), undated (ca. 1938).
Oil and pencil on paperboard, 20 x 15-1/16 (sheet).
Lent by the National Collection of Fine Arts, Smithsonian Institution.

SEYMOUR FOGEL

45. Sketch for REHABILITATION, undated (ca. 1938) (mural for entrance lobby, WPA Building).
Tempera on illustration board, 7½ x 8¼ (sight).
Lent by Mrs. Seymour Fogel.

Guston, Refregier, and Fogel were among a group of six master artists and numerous assistants assigned by the Federal Art Project to decorate the WPA Building. Stylistically, the murals were among the most advanced of the figurative works which predominated at the Fair, representing a synthesis of elements from Mexican, Renaissance, and Cubist sources. All the murals expressed the theme, "Work – The American Way," for the building was dedicated to proving that the WPA was the way "out of enforced idleness for millions in all walks of life."

In a popularity poll conducted by the Mural Artists Guild in August of 1939, the WPA Building captured two of the four top prizes, with Guston's work taking first place in the outdoor category and Refregier's coming second in the indoor classification. In her comments on the awards, Ruth Green Harris, art critic of The New York Times, praised the Guston mural: "In a clear and positive statement, Guston has given visual form to a strongly felt abstract idea. The composition is magnificent; content and form inseparable." She wrote of Refregier in similar terms: "the excellent compositions are simpler and clearer than any explanatory words. In each panel form and purpose are inseparable, and this unity so apparent in each is the result of an idea of which the mural is the visual expression." (July 28, 1940)

Seymour Fogel at work on "Rehabilitation," February 1939. (WPA — HAH)

Augusta Savage presents a scale model of "The Harp" to Grover Whalen. (NYP)

AUGUSTA SAVAGE

46. THE HARP ("LIFT EVERY VOICE AND SING"), undated (ca. 1938) (model of forecourt sculpture, Contemporary Arts Building).
White metal alloy, 10½ x 4 x 9¼.
Signed on base: Augusta Savage.
Lent by Barry Kogan.

Augusta Savage was the only black artist to receive a commission from the Fair Corporation; although there was an official policy of non-discrimination in hiring, few blacks worked at the Fair in any other than a menial capacity. In response to inquiries from the Urban League, the Board of Directors noted that the Fair was "according recognition" to Negroes, and cited the promotion of a porter, Walter Roberts, to the design staff and the Savage commission as examples of this recognition. (See Executive Committee Minutes, Feb. 28, 1938.) However, the Fair did also commission the distinguished black composer, William Grant Still, to create the symphonic theme, "The Rising Tide," for the Democracity exhibit.

THE HARP represents a choir supported by the arm and hand of the Creator. The kneeling figure holds the first bar of James Weldon Johnson's "Lift Every Voice and Sing," the so-called "Negro national anthem." The full-scale version of the sculpture, in painted plaster, stood at the Rainbow Avenue entrance to the Contemporary Arts Building (called American Art Today in 1940).

GORDON W. GILKEY

47. CONTEMPORARY AMERICAN ART
    BUILDING, Undated (1938).
    Etching and soft-ground, 5½ x 7⅜ (image).
    Monogrammed in plate, signed in pencil.
    Lent by the Library of Congress.

48. HALL OF FASHION, undated (1938).
    Etching and aquatint, 7⅜ x 8¾ (image).
    Signed in pencil.
    Lent by the Library of Congress.

42.

Philip Guston, "Maintaining America's Skills,"
WPA Building. (NSS)

39. "Fountain of the Atom," Bowling Green. (HB)

Mural by Willem De Kooning, north wall,
Hall of Pharmacy. (PMW)

ILYA BOLOTOWSKY

49. Study for mural, Hall of Medicine and
Public Health, undated (ca. 1938).
Casein, ink, and pencil on illustration
board, 10½ x 22.
Lent by the artist.

LOUIS SCHANKER

50. Study for mural, Hall of Medicine and
Public Health, undated (1938).
Oil on canvas, 10½ x 25.
Lent by Mr. and Mrs. Martin Diamond.

51. Preliminary sketch for mural, Hall of
Medicine and Public Health, 1938.
Pencil and watercolor on illustration
board, 5 x 12½ (image).
Signed and dated, lower right: Schanker '38.
Lent by Martin Diamond Fine Arts, New York.

Ilya Bolotowsky with a sketch for his
abstract mural, Hall of Medicine and Public
Health. (FVO'C)

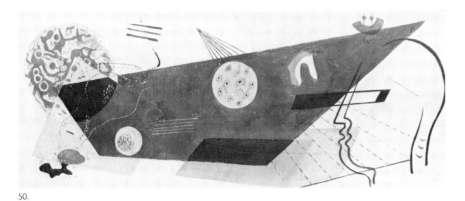

50.

"Pharmacy from the Beginning," by
Stuyvesant Van Veen, Hall of Pharmacy. (SVV)

52. SECOND SKETCH FOR 39 WORLD'S FAIR, 1938.
Pencil and watercolor on illustration board, 7 x 14.
Signed and dated, lower right: Schanker '38.
Lent by Martin Diamond Fine Arts, New York.

53. MURAL SKETCH 1939 WORLD'S FAIR, 1938.
Pencil and watercolor on illustration board, 9½ x 14⅞.
Signed and dated, lower right: Schanker '38.
Lent by Martin Diamond Fine Arts, New York.

BALCOMB GREENE

54. BLUE WORLD (sketch for mural, Hall of Medicine and Public Health), undated (1938).
Casein tempera on masonite, 24 x 37¼.
Lent by the artist

BYRON BROWNE

55. Sketch for mural, Hall of Medicine and Public Health, undated (1938).
Pencil and watercolor on illustration board, 3⅝ x 7¼.
Lent by Frank Cronican.

The four abstract murals in the Hall of Medicine and Public Health were executed under the WPA Federal Art Project, with the sponsorship of the American Medical Association. Three figurative panels on the history of medicine by Abraham Lishinsky and Irving Block, and three photomurals by Alexander Alland and Leo Lances, were also done under WPA auspices.

All four of the muralists were members of the American Abstract Artists (Greene was its chairman), a group formed in 1936 to champion the cause of native abstraction. That their work should have been characterized in Parnassus, *a leading art magazine, as "uncomplicated" and a "psychological relief" for viewers illustrates the widespread lack of appreciation of their achievement during the 1930s.*

STUYVESANT VAN VEEN

56. PHARMACY FROM THE BEGINNING (sketch for mural, Hall of Pharmacy), 1937.
Oil pastel on illustration board, 27½ x 35⅛.
Lent by Mr. and Mrs. Stuyvesant Van Veen

Browne mural in situ, Hall of Medicine and Public Health. (WPA — HAH)

Sketch for mural by Byron Browne, mounted for presentation. (SB)

54.

"Production," by Michael Loew, Hall of Pharmacy. (ML)

MICHAEL LOEW

57. PRODUCTION, final sketch, undated (early 1939).
Tempera on masonite, 21¾ x 69.
Signed, lower right: Michael Loew.
Lent by the artist.

The Hall of Pharmacy originally was designed as a Production Building and was therefore not in the correct thematic sector, being located on the Court of Power in the Production and Distribution zone. Michael Loew, whose mural decorated the entrance façade, planned his work to reflect the original theme. The two other muralists, Stuyvesant Van Veen and Willem de Kooning, came to the project later and executed designs related to the theme of pharmacy.

In Loew's PRODUCTION, symbols of natural and mechanical power are integrated with figures representing both allegorical personifications of natural forces and specific depictions of the worker and the family. Van Veen's composition is dominated by the modern chemistry associated with pharmaceutical research, contrasting with the figure of the alchemist, who symbolizes the superstitious practices of early pharmacists. De Kooning's mural, one of the most prominent and striking at the Fair, was on the building's curving northwest wall. Stylistic similarities can be seen in the work of Loew and de Kooning, but, unfortunately, no sketches for the latter's huge mural are known to have survived.

FRANK CRONICAN

58. Model of Medicine and Public Health, Science and Education Building (Mayers, Murray and Phillip, architects).
Mixed media, in plexiglas case, 4 x 7¾ x 8½.
Lent by Frank Cronican.

GORDON W. GILKEY

59. MEDICINE AND PUBLIC HEALTH BUILDING, undated (1938).
Etching, 8¾ x 6¼ (image).
Monogrammed in plate; signed in pencil.
Lent by the Library of Congress.

60. HALL OF PHARMACY, undated (1938).
Etching, 8¾ x 5⅜ (image).
Signed in pencil.
Lent by the Library of Congress.

Heinz pickle pin, 1939 model. Lent by
Arthur Cohen. (AL)

**LEONARD M. SCHULTZE AND
ARCHIBALD M. BROWN, architects**

61. FOOD BUILDING 06 (Heinz Dome), 1937.
Watercolor and pencil on illustration
board, 30 x 40.
Dated June 20, 1937.
Lent by the Museum of the City
of New York.

*The Heinz Dome was a Fair-built structure
leased by Heinz and attached to the Academy
of Sport; it was originally designated as the
Fisheries exhibit. The mural on the facade,
Triumphant Poseidon, by Domenico Mortellito,
reflects the building's original theme, while the
decorations on the dome, Harvest — Occidental
and Oriental, by the same artist, treated a
subject more closely related to the building's
final function as a food pavilion.*

*The interior of the dome featured the
Fair's largest sculptural construction, a sixty-
five-foot fountain decorated with statuary and
crowned by the sixteen-foot Goddess of
Perfection. In 1940, the Goddess was moved
outside to the pinnacle of the dome. In its
display Heinz demonstrated soil-less
hydroponic cultivation in the Garden of the*

Heinz Dome, 1940. (Heinz)

Rotunda, Food Building North, mural by
Pierre Bourdelle. (FC)

Borden's "Dairy World of Tomorrow," with
heads of Elsie the Cow punctuating the
rotunda. (HB)

Future, and gave away its famous pickle pin
(introduced at the 1893 World's Columbian
Exposition). In 1940 it was estimated that 6
million pickle pins had been distributed at the
New York World's Fair.

ASPINWALL, SIMPSON AND DEL GAUDIO, architects

62. FOOD BUILDING N7 (Food Building
North), 1937.
Watercolor and pencil on illustration
board, 28 x 44; approved July 6, 1937.
Lent by the Museum of the City of
New York.

63. Rendering of north elevation, Food
Building North, undated (ca. 1937).
Pastel on paper, 12 x 36.
Lent by the Museum of the City of
New York.

64. Rendering of south elevation, Food
Building North, undated (ca. 1937).
Pastel on paper 14½ x 38½.
Lent by the Museum of the City of
New York.

*Facing the Heinz Dome across Constitution
Mall, Food North featured a rotunda decorated
by Pierre Bourdelle. Murals on the courtyard
façade were by Carlo Ciampaglia. A third food
building, facing Lincoln Square, housed the
zone's focal exhibit by Russell Wright. Coca-
Cola was the main exhibitor and in 1940 took
over the entire building, with the exception of
the focal exhibit space.*

FRANK CRONICAN

65. Model of Heinz Dome.
Mixed media, in plexiglas case, 3½ x 10 x 8.
Lent by Frank Cronican.

66. Model of Food Building North.
Mixed media, in plexiglas case,
3¾ x 7 x 10½.
Lent by Frank Cronican.

VOORHEES, GMELIN AND WALKER, architects

67. TEMPLATE AND ELEVATIONS FOR
COWS HEADS, BORDEN PAVILION,
1938.
Pencil on tracing paper, 26¼ x 37½.
Dated, lower right: October 18, 1938.
Lent by Haines, Lundberg and Waehler,
courtesy of Spaced Gallery, New York.

Night view of the Continental Baking
Company Building. (HB)

VOORHEES, WALKER, FOLEY AND SMITH, architects

68. TO THE BULLS (study for directional sign), 1939.
Pencil on tracing paper, 16¾ x 25¾.
Dated, lower right: April 20, 1939.
Lent by Haines, Lundberg and Waehler, courtesy of Spaced Gallery, New York.

69. TO THE ROTOLACTOR (study for directional sign), 1939.
Pencil on tracing paper, 18 x 27⅞.
Dated, lower right: April 20, 1939.
Lent by Haines, Lundberg and Waehler, courtesy of Spaced Gallery, New York.

The main attraction at the Dairy World of Tomorrow was the Walker-Gordon Rotolactor, on which five pedigreed cows were shower-bathed, dried with sterilized towels, and mechanically milked on a revolving platform, demonstrating "the modern hygienic methods of milking that may be used universally in the future for the benefit of mankind." The milk was then processed and bottled on the premises.

In a promotional brochure, the building's architects stated that:

> *Decorative motifs whimsically extolled bovine charm in the personage of Elsie the Cow, a symbol introduced at the fair that has subsequently acquired national recognition. Three-dimensional portraits of Elsie, executed in copper by Giovanni Repetto, adorned the rim of the gold-surfaced pavilion cylinder. The main display area also was grandly dominated by Elsie and her Milky Way. Continuing with this theme, the product display cases in a Hall of Dioramas were covered in cowhide and suspended by leather thongs from yokes on the ceiling.*

GORDON W. GILKEY

70. THE FOOD BUILDING (Food Building North), undated (1938).
Etching and soft-ground, 7 x 8⅞ (image).
Monogrammed in plate, signed in pencil.
Lent by the Library of Congress.

71. FOOD FOCAL EXHIBIT HALL, undated (1938).
Etching and soft-ground, 8⅞ x 6⅞ (image).
Signed in pencil.
Lent by the Library of Congress.

72. HEINZ DOME, undated (1938).
Etching, 6⅜ x 8¾ (image).
Signed in pencil.
Lent by the Library of Congress.

73. CONTINENTAL BAKING COMPANY, undated (1938).
Etching and soft-ground, 5⅞ x 7⅞ (image).
Signed in pencil.
Lent by the Library of Congress.

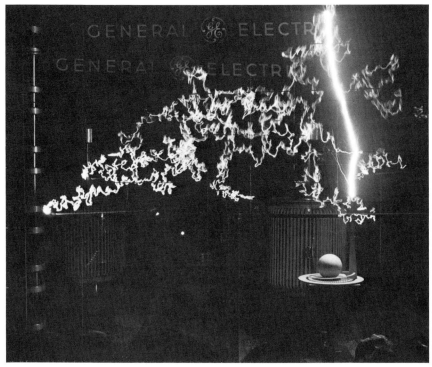

Man-made lightning electrified visitors
to GE's Steinmetz Hall. (Sam Fox)

FRANK CRONICAN

74. Model of Electric Utilities Building
(Harrison & Fouilhoux, architects).
Mixed media, in plexiglas case, 4 x 8 x 7½.
Lent by Frank Cronican.

75. Model of General Electric Building
(Voorhees, Walker, Foley & Smith,
architects).
Mixed media, in plexiglas case, 3½ x 7 x 8.
Lent by Frank Cronican.

VOORHEES, GMELIN AND
WALKER, architects

76. General Electric Building, south elevation,
undated (ca. 1937).
Pencil and colored pencil on illustration
board, 20 x 30.
Lent by the Museum of the City
of New York.

General Electric's "Lightning Bolt" tower. (MR)

ROCKWELL KENT

77. Mural for General Electric Building,
1938-39 (oil on canvas?), destroyed.
Color photograph, 6 x 19¾.
Lent by Allen L. Palanker.

*Kent's mural was located in the General
Electric House of Magic, the auditorium in
which startling developments in electrical
research were demonstrated. Its subject matter
—the influence of electricity in providing
comforts, conveniences, and higher living
standards for the American people—was
described in a GE brochure as follows:*

> *At the left the mural depicts the
> superstitions and misbeliefs of the Dark
> Ages—the alchemists, astrologers,
> philosophers, and witches. Then, with the
> coming of electricity (symbolized by two
> heroic figures), progress and enlightenment
> come to the world. Under the influence of
> its liberating power, the toilers of the world
> are shown discarding their outmoded tools
> and marching on to the more abundant life,
> represented by the city of the future.*

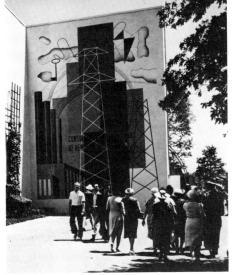

Mural by Fernand Leger, Con Edison Building, north wall. (Con. Ed.)

Consolidated Edison Building. (PMW)

Electrical Products (Means of Distribution) Building. (HB)

FERNAND LÉGER

78. Preliminary sketches for mural or fountain, Consolidated Edison Building, undated (1938).
Pencil on paper, 12¾ x 17⅝ (sight).
Lent by the Herbert F. Johnson Museum of Art, Cornell University, Ithaca, New York.

79. Sketch for mural, Consolidated Edison Building, undated (1938).
Pencil on paper, 10¾ x 8.
Lent by Mr. and Mrs. Charles V. Hooks.

80. Sketch for mural, Consolidated Edison Building, undated (1938).
Colored pencil on paper, 10¾ x 8½.
Lent by Mr. and Mrs. Charles V. Hooks.

81. Sketch for mural, Consolidated Edison Building, undated (1938).
Watercolor on paper, 10¼ x 8¾.
Lent by Mr. and Mrs. Charles V. Hooks.

Léger came to the United States in 1938, when he was commissioned to decorate the apartment of Nelson Rockeller. His work was well known to Wallace Harrison, architect of the Consolidated Edison Building, who was instrumental in securing the Fair commission for Léger. The artist executed many thumbnail sketches in the offices of Harrison and Fouilhoux; his final design was scaled up on the wall by union workmen.

Writing of the sketches at the time of their exhibition at the Herbert F. Johnson Museum in 1978, Deborah Solomon points out that:

The Westinghouse "Singing Tower of Light." (GK)

Léger's fascination with machine parts and reverence for efficiency makes his collaboration with Con Ed unsurprising. The block-long pavilion, complete with miniature trains speeding through subways, elevators rising and descending in skyscrapers, and traffic flowing across suspension bridges, affirms Léger's view that hope for the future lies in technology's innovations. . . . In the finished Consolidated Edison mural, Benjamin Franklin's symbolic kite and key float amid amorphous clouds as if they were a part of nature. Similarly, a sun with rays like metal prongs could belong to the power plant behind it. Sinuous curves that might have delineated classical nudes in Ingres's paintings, almost a century earlier, are used by Léger to indicate both

power plants and green plants. Nature and technology become unified in an organic interpretation of a world redeemed through scientific progress. (Fernand Léger: Mural Sketches, p. 3.)

WALKER AND GILLETTE, architects

82. MEANS OF DISTRIBUTION BUILDING V3 (Electrical Products Building), undated (ca. 1937).
Watercolor and pencil on illustration board, 30 x 40.
Lent by the Museum of the City of New York.

GORDON W. GILKEY

83. ELECTRICAL PRODUCTS BUILDING, undated (1938).
Etching and soft-ground, $8\frac{7}{8}$ x $7\frac{3}{8}$ (image).
Signed in pencil.
Lent by the Library of Congress.

84. HALL OF THE PETROLEUM INDUSTRY, undated (1938).
Etching and aquatint, $7\frac{1}{8}$ x $8\frac{3}{4}$ (image).
Monogrammed in plate, signed in pencil.
Lent by the Library of Congress.

85. DU PONT'S WONDER WORLD OF CHEMISTRY, undated (1938).
Etching and aquatint, $6\frac{7}{8}$ x $8\frac{3}{4}$ (image).
Monogrammed in plate, signed in pencil.
Lent by the Library of Congress.

Du Pont's Wonder World of Chemistry. (HB)

86.

DAVENPORT HOSIERY MILLS,
manufacturers

86. Nylon stocking, showing pre-War deniers.
Du Pont nylon yarn, length 35.
Lent by E. I. Du Pont de Nemours, Inc.

*The development of Nylon fiber was
announced to the public on October 27, 1938,
in confirmation of rumors that had been
circulating in the textile industry for several
months.* Popular Mechanics *described the
substance as "a combination of coal, air, and
water. It is a protein-like chemical, somewhat
resembling silk, hair, and wool in composition,
but actually unlike anything found in nature."
Initially, the fiber was used in brushes and was
shown at the Fair as toothbrush bristles and
fishing line. There were also displays of the
experimental use of Nylon in knitwear and
hosiery, although commercial production did
not begin until December 1939.*

*Other important Du Pont displays
included Lucite, a methyl methacrylate plastic
that had been developed in 1936, Plastacele
and Cellophane, the weaving of Rayon yarn,
and demonstrations of new products being
developed by Du Pont research.*

Interior display, Du Pont Building. (WDT)

TRANSPORTATION

Crosley motorcade, June 1939.
(Crosley Auto Club)

CROSLEY CORPORATION, manufacturers

87. Automobile, Crosley coupe convertible, 1941.
Two-cylinder, air-cooled, 12 h.p. engine, gasoline operated.
Length 120, tread 48.
Lent by Harold Serva.

Powel Crosley, Jr. began to experiment with his concept of a small, economical, lightweight car in 1911. It was not until 1937, however, that a practical model was developed; and on April 28, 1939 the Crosley Car of Tomorrow was introduced at the Indianapolis Speedway. In June a motorcade of Crosley cars, piloted by an all-girl driving team, paraded across the George Washington Bridge to the Crosley pavilion at the Fair. (Because the Crosley Corporation was primarily a manufacturer of radios, its building was located in the Communications zone.)

In the car's promotional booklet, Crosley reminded potential buyers that "In recent years the trend in motor cars has been toward bigger, faster, more powerful gasoline consumers. Economic conditions, however, make it essential that we give some attention to mileage per gallon and operating cost and possible economies."

Designed to sell cheaply (like Crosley radios and refrigerators), to run economically (like Crosley's Cincinnati Reds), the new four-passenger car has a two-seater companion, a convertible coupe which can also be used as a quarter-ton delivery truck.... The new car has... a high speed of fifty miles an hour, and runs fifty to sixty miles on a gallon of gasoline. Two quarts of oil fill its crankcase, four gallons of gas its fuel tank. At $325 for the coupe, $25 more for the sedan, it will undersell by $62 the only other U. S. midget on the automotive market, the American Bantam. (Time, May 8, 1939.)

NORMAN BEL GEDDES, designer

88. FUTURAMA: Key plan for model layout with descriptive tables, undated.
Blue-line print, 49¼ x 40.
Lent by the Norman Bel Geddes Collection, Hoblitzelle Theatre Arts Library, Humanities Research Center, University of Texas, Austin.

89. FUTURAMA: Selection of scale model vehicles.
Passenger car, painted metal, 6 x 6 x 3.
Bus, metal, 13½ x 3½ x 3½.
Double-decker bus, painted metal, 13½ x 4½ x 4.
Two commercial delivery vehicles, painted metal, each 7 x 2½ x 2¼.
Lent by the Norman Bel Geddes Collection, Hoblitzelle Theatre Arts Library, Humanities Research Center, University of Texas, Austin.

90. FUTURAMA: Selection of extruded plastic small-scale vehicles.
Lent by Robert Gaston Herbert II.

91. FUTURAMA: Four figures from the Street of Tomorrow
Cast lead, height 3.
Lent by Robert Gaston Herbert II.

92. FUTURAMA: Four model suburban homes.
Unpainted wood and brass, basic module 2 x 2½ x 1¾.
Lent by Robert Gaston Herbert II.

FUTURAMA, designed by Norman Bel Geddes, working with a team of consultants, engineers, technicians, and a staff of 700 artists and craftsmen, was the single most popular exhibit at the Fair, attracting an estimated 25 million visitors. As Bel Geddes noted in his 1940 book, Magic Motorways, "the reason its popularity never diminished was that its boldness was based on soundness. The plan it presented appealed to the practical engineer as well as to the idle day-dreamer. The motorways which it featured were not only desirable, but practical." (p. 6).

The 35,000 square foot panoramic model was actually a series of 408 separate sections in several scales, designed to simulate a trip across the country by air. Viewers sat in a moving chair-train of 552 cars, each with individually synchronized speakers, having the capacity to carry 28,000 visitors daily on their 1/3-mile trip around the America of 1960. The souvenir booklet reminded passengers that "the FUTURAMA...is designed, not as a projection of any particular highway plan or program, but rather to demonstrate in dramatic fashion that the world, far from being finished, is hardly yet begun; that the job of building the future is one which will demand our best energies, our most fruitful imagination; and that with it will come greater opportunities for all."

In Life's feature story on FUTURAMA (June 5, 1939), some of the model's more startling features were pointed out, and the quality of life twenty years into the World of Tomorrow was outlined:

The land is really greener than it was in 1939....Men love their fields and gardens better and more wisely.

The cars, built like raindrops, are powered by rear engines that are probably improvements of the Diesel. Inside, they are air-conditioned. They cost as low as $200.

Liquid air is by 1960 a potent, mobile source of power. Atomic energy is being used cautiously.

It is important to remember that the people of 1960 have more time, more energy, and more tools to have fun.

The aspect of FUTURAMA that made the most significant impression on visitors was the arterial highway system—understandably the major focus of an exhibit by an automobile manufacturer. The model was interlaced with seven-lane superhighways with radio control towers, designed to accommodate traffic at speeds of up to 100-miles-per-hour. Tube lighting, built into the safety curbs, provided even, continuous illumination at night. The outmoded cloverleaf intersection was eliminated, replaced by high-speed entry ramps enabling turns at fifty miles per hour. Cantilevered roadways clinging to mountainsides and a spectacular catenary suspension bridge, supported by a single giant cable, led to a streamlined metropolis in which vehicular and pedestrian traffic were safely isolated on separate levels. At the ride's end, this dream of a perfectly integrated city of "space, sunshine, light, and air" became a reality as visitors stepped from their chairs into a full-scale version of the model intersection over which they had just "flown."

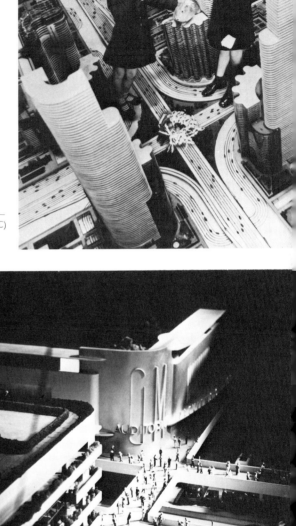

An Easter treat—
a visit to Futurama. (FC)

"Futurama" intersection with large-scale vehicles and three-inch figures. (BGA)

96.

GORDON W. GILKEY

93. MARINE TRANSPORTATION
BUILDING, undated (1938).
Etching and soft-ground, 8⅞ x 7½ (image).
Monogrammed in plate, signed in pencil.
Lent by the Library of Congress.

ELI JACQUES KAHN,
MUSCHENHEIM AND BROUNN,
architects.

94. Plans and elevations, Marine
Transportation Building, undated (ca.
1937).
Pencil and airbrush on illustration board,
30 x 40.
Lent by the Museum of the City
of New York.

DESIGNER UNKNOWN

95. PERSPECTIVE STUDY OF INTERIOR
SPACE FOR U. S. LINES, 1937.
Pencil, watercolor, and airbrush on
illustration board, with photostat of
building plan, 20 x 27¾.
Dated, center right: December 28, 1937.
Lent by the Museum of the City
of New York.

LYONEL FEININGER

96. Design for mural, Marine Transportation
Building, undated (1938).
Watercolor and ink on paper, 3-5/16 x
10¼.
Lent by Marlborough Fine Arts
(London) Ltd.

97. Sketch for mural, Marine Transportation
Building, undated (1938).
Watercolor and ink on paper, 3-11/16 x
12¼.
Lent by Marlborough Fine Arts
(London) Ltd.

Greyhound vehicles in Bowling Green.
(PMW)

98. Sketch for mural, Marine Transportation
Building, 1938.
Watercolor and ink on paper, 6-11/16 x
24-13/16.
Signed and dated, lower left: Feininger
1938.
Lent by Marlborough Fine Arts
(London) Ltd.

*Feininger, an American artist who had
emigrated to Germany in 1887, had been a
leading member of the avant-garde in Europe
during the period of pre-war experimentation
and a faculty member of the Bauhaus during
the 1920s and 30s. In 1936 he returned to the
United States, where he remained until his
death in 1957. His work is characterized by the
dynamic fragmentation of form, derived from a
synthesis of Cubist, Orphist, and Futurist styles,
and frequently reflects his interest in music and
the power and drama of natural forces.*

*The sea and ships are subjects that
constantly reappear in Feininger's work and
maritime themes form a significant portion of
his oeuvre. (A series of studies of sailing vessels
from the mid-30s prefigures the Marine
Transportation mural both stylistically and
conceptually.) The mural, occupying a wall 25'
by 120' on the building's façade, is in fact a
series of five vignettes, each of which contains
a complete composition. Four sailing vessels
and a modern ocean liner express the theme,
Shipping Old and New.*

RAYMOND LOEWY, designer

99. Design for Greyhound intramural bus,
1938.
Airbrush and metallic paint on illustration
board, 12 x 24¾.
Signed and dated on mat, lower right:
Loewy '38.
Lent by the Museum of the City of
New York.

*One hundred intramural buses, seating forty-
eight, made thirty-two stops around the
periphery of the Fairgrounds at 10¢ a ride.
Greyhound also operated fifty three- and four-
car tractor trains costing 25¢, which
meandered around the grounds at 3—4 miles
an hour for sightseeing. Single and double
push-chairs, operated by the American Express
Company, could be hired for from fifty cents to
one dollar for fifteen minutes.*

99.

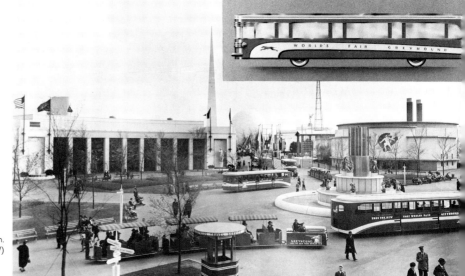

Chrysler Motors Building. (PMW)

WALTER DORWIN TEAGUE,
designer

100. Garden plan, Ford Building, 1938.
Pencil and colored pencil on paper,
mounted on illustration board, 20 x 23.
Dated, verso: March 4, 1938.
Lent by the Museum of the City
of New York.

DESIGNER UNKNOWN

101. Plan of fountains at base of EUROPA
statue, Court of Railroads, undated
(ca. 1938).
Tempera on black illustration board,
27⅞ x 22.
Lent by the Museum of the City
of New York.

GLEB DERUJINSKY

102. EUROPA (pedestal version of sculpture,
Court of Railroads), undated.
Marble, 15 x 21⅜ x 8½.
Signed on base: G. Derujinsky.
Lent by Mrs. Gleb Derujinsky, courtesy of
Graham Galleries, New York.

Ford's "Road of Tomorrow." (WDT)

EUROPA, situated in front of the Railroads Building, was one of the numerous monumental sculptures on the Fairgrounds and among the most photogenic. The subject, taken from mythology, is a Phoenician princess being carried across the sea by Zeus, who had assumed the form of a white bull. It was described by Life (March 13, 1939) as "one of the most famous transportation feats of all time."

JAMES GAMBREL ROGERS, architect

103. West elevation, Chrysler Motors Building (Transportation focal), undated (ca. 1937). Pencil, watercolor, and airbrush on illustration board, 16 x 40. Lent by the Museum of the City of New York.

The Chrysler Building was designed for the Fair Corporation as the Transportation focal

exhibit, which occupied the rotunda of the pavilion. The striking and innovative mobile Polaroid mural by Henry Billings above the main entrance was, for reasons presently unknown, covered over or removed in 1940.

EMRICH NICHOLSON, designer

104. Steamlined car design for flag, 1938. Pencil and tempera on illustration board, 9 x 12 (image). Signed and dated, lower right: Emrich Nicholson/May 1938. Lent by the Museum of the City of New York.

105. Steam engine design for flag, 1938. Pencil and tempera on illustration board, 9 x 12 (image). Signed and dated, lower right: Emrich Nicholson/May 1938. Lent by the Museum of the City of New York.

102.

"Europa," with the General Motors Building in the background. (PMW)

GOVERNMENT

President Roosevelt addresses crowds of Fair workers and visitors at the official opening ceremonies, April 30, 1939. (PMW)

In June 1936 President Roosevelt was authorized by Congress to invite the nations of the world to participate in the Fair; and in December Governor Lehman of New York extended the invitation to the states. In all sixty foreign governments and international bodies and thirty-three states and territories were represented. In May of 1937 the Paris-based Bureau International des Expositions recognized the Fair as the official international exposition for 1939.

The Official Guide Book proclaimed that "the presence of sixty foreign participants makes the Fair a true parliament of the world. Here the peoples of the world unite in amity and understanding, impelled by a friendly rivalry, and working toward a common purpose: to set forth their achievements of today and their contributions to the World of Tomorrow. The Fair is a force for peace in the world; for without peace the dream of a better World of Tomorrow is but a cruel and mocking illusion."

The most notable absentee was Germany, which had in fact contracted for a pavilion in 1937, amid protests from anti-Nazi groups. However, in April of 1938, the German Consul

General informed Grover Whalen that his government could not raise sufficient foreign exchange to proceed with construction and was withdrawing from the Fair. (See Executive Committee Minutes, January 10 and May 2, 1938.) China was also without an official exhibit but was represented in the Amusement zone by a replica of the Holy Potala-Su (Golden Temple) of Jehol, also shown at the Century of Progress exposition in Chicago. Japan, then at war with China, erected a handsome pavilion modeled on a Shinto shrine, complete with formal gardens. Japan and several other foreign exhibitors had both independent pavilions and displays in the free exhibit space provided by the Fair Corporation in the Hall of Nations, a pair of buildings which flanked the Court of Peace.

GORDON W. GILKEY

106. U.S. GOVERNMENT BUILDING AND HALLS OF NATIONS, undated (1938). Etching, 7⅜ x 8⅞ (image). Monogrammed in plate, signed in pencil. Lent by the Library of Congress.

FRANK CRONICAN

107. Model of the United States Government Building. (Howard L. Cheney, architect.) Mixed media, in plexiglas case, 3½ x 8¼ x 6¾. Lent by Frank Cronican.

CONCETTA SCARAVAGLIONE

108. WOMAN WITH MOUNTAIN SHEEP (maquette for sculpture in Garden Court, United States Government Building), undated (ca. 1938). Painted plaster, height 42. Lent by the Public Buildings Service, General Services Administration.

MARION WALTON

109. MAN WITH CALF (maquette for sculpture in Garden Court, United States Government Building), undated (ca. 1938). Painted plaster, height 42. Lent by the Public Buildings Service, General Services Administration.

The Federal exhibits included numerous specially commissioned works of art, many of

Aeriel view, Government zone. (MCNY)

which were allocated to government agencies at the close of the Fair. The maquettes on exhibition are for two of six plaster figures which stood against the semicircular wall of the Garden Court and which were demolished with the building. Their style reflects the massive, simplified forms common to much of the monumental and architectural sculpture of the period.

FRANK CRONICAN

110. Model of the French Pavilion (Expert & Patout, architects).
Mixed media, in plexiglas case, 3¼ x 6¾ x 6.
Lent by Frank Cronican.

111. Model of the Russian Pavilion (Simon Breines, Boris M. Iofan & Karo S. Albain, architects).
Mixed media, in plexiglas case, 6¼ x 8 x 8¾.
Lent by Frank Cronican.

PHOTOGRAPHER UNKNOWN

112. THE RUSSIAN PAVILION AT THE 1939 WORLD'S FAIR, undated (1938-39).
Photographs with typed captions, bound, 24 x 20 inches.
Lent by Charles Apfelbaum Books, Valley Stream, N.Y.

The Soviet Union, the first major foreign exhibitor to sign a contract for space at the Fair, erected a pavilion covered in pink marble and topped by a 79' stainless steel statue of a worker holding aloft a red star. Irreverently dubbed Big Joe, the statue made the building the tallest structure at the Fair with the exception of the Trylon. The building was

dismantled in the winter of 1939 and shipped back to the Soviet Union. In 1940 its place was taken by the American Common, where patriotic pageants, musical programs, and performances were staged.

YORK AND SAWYER, architects

113. COURT OF STATES COLONIAL SECTOR, SPANISH BUILDINGS, KEY ELEVATIONS, 1938.
Pencil on tracing paper, 29⅞ x 42½.
Dated, lower right: August 3, 1938.
Lent by the Department of Parks, City of New York.

114. COURT OF STATES COLONIAL SECTOR, SPANISH BUILDINGS, TOWER ELEVATIONS AND DETAILS, 1938.
Pencil on tracing paper, 29⅞ x 42.
Dated, lower right: August 3, 1938.
Lent by the Department of Parks, City of New York.

LAWRENCE G. WHITE, JAMES K. SMITH, FREDERIC P. KING, associated architects

115. COURT OF STATES, INDEPENDENCE HALL—BLDG #14, UPPER PART OF TOWER AND SECTION A³-A³, 1938.
Pencil on tracing paper, 30 x 42.
Dated, lower right: August 22, 1938.
Lent by the Department of Parks, City of New York.

The Court of States was the only sector of the Fair where historical styles in architecture were permitted by the Board of Design. Several states erected replicas of noted landmarks within their borders, such as Pennsylvania's Independence Hall, New Jersey's Trenton Barracks, and the Alamo of Texas.

108.

France. (PMW)

GORDON W. GILKEY

116. CONSTRUCTION, NEW YORK CITY BUILDING, undated (1938).
Etching, 8⅞ x 6⅞ (image).
Monogrammed in plate, signed in pencil.
Lent by the Library of Congress.

117. NEW YORK CITY BUILDING, undated (1938).
Etching, 6 x 7⅞ (image).
Monogrammed in plate, signed in pencil.
Lent by the Library of Congress.

J. J. WENNER, architectural model makers

118. Model of the New York City Building, undated (ca. 1937) (Aymar Embury II, architect).
Mixed media, in plate glass case, 19 x 67 x 36¾.
The Queens Museum.

The City Building was constructed as a permanent recreation facility as well as a Fair pavilion containing the exhibits of the various municipal agencies. The original plan featured a two-story roofed court surrounded by a balcony; this arrangement is still visible in the south wing. At the time of construction roller

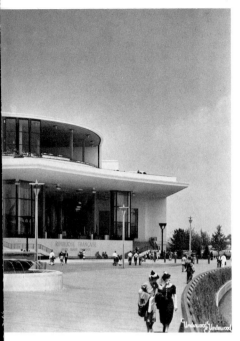

and ice rinks were installed but were covered during the Fair. During the war these facilities were opened to the public.

From 1946-1950 the building was the annual meeting place of the United Nations General Assembly, and from 1952-1962 was again used as a recreation center. The north wing was converted for city exhibits at the 1964-1965 World's Fair, for which the 18,000-square foot Panorama of the City of New York was constructed. After housing displays by the Triborough Bridge and Tunnel Authority from 1966-1970, the north wing became the home of The Queens Museum in November 1972.

New York City Building. (PMW)

AMUSEMENTS

A "Living Magazine Cover" for a publication of the future. (AS)

"A is for amusement; and in the interests of many of the millions of Fair visitors amusement comes first. Historically, fairs have always been associated with festivals and celebrations. The Amusement zone covers 280 acres — an area larger than the entire Paris Exposition of 1937. Here the Fair presents streamlined festivity for the World of Today and for the World of Tomorrow." (Official Souvenir Book)

NEMBHARD N. CULIN

119. Study for Amusement area lighting canopy, undated (ca. 1938).
Pencil and colored pencil on paper, mounted on illustration board, 11¾ x 15½ (sheet).
Signed, lower right: Culin.
Lent by the artist.

GORDON W. GILKEY

120. THE PARACHUTE JUMP, undated (1938).
Etching and soft-ground, 8⅞ x 6 (image).
Monogrammed in plate, signed in pencil.
Lent by the Library of Congress.

"There was fun to be had at the Parachute Jump, an instant and lasting favorite at forty cents a jump. This exciting attraction was one of the most publicized and biggest novelties at the fair. It was the invention of Commander Strong, U.S.N. (retired). He had been a Navy aviator for over twenty years, and upon his retirement, on his estate at Hightstown, New Jersey, he put up a device calculated to give all and sundry the sensations hitherto reserved for a few select members of the Caterpillar Club.

After experimenting with wires and pulleys in 1934, he finally perfected an arrangement whereby one might drop to earth under the protecting canopy of a parachute without the danger of breaking one's neck. It was used by sailors and soldiers in training, and its commercial appeal was responsible for getting it to Flushing Meadow. At the fair it grossed over $350,000, was sponsored by Life Savers Corporation, and was operated by the Safe Parachute Jump Company.

"The ride, a steel structure 250 feet high (360 feet to the tip of the flagpole), became the prototype for the parachute jumps at Fort Benning, Georgia, and other places where the armed forces train their parachute troops. At a distance the jump with its chutes going up and down looks like a giant yo-yo. It was the largest and highest amusement ride in the world, and over a half a million visitors took the 'jump' at Flushing Meadow. It is now located at Coney Island."

(From World's Fair Midways *by Edo McCullough, © 1966 Carnivaland Enterprises, Inc., published by Exposition Press, Inc., Smithtown, N. Y.)*

HAMMOND ORGAN COMPANY, manufacturers

121. NOVACHORD electric keyboard instrument, undated (ca. 1939).
Wood veneer case, 40 x 52 x 37.
Lent by Rachel Elkind, Tempi Productions

The Novachord, invented by Laurens Hammond, was given its first public demonstration in New York two months prior to the Fair. As reported in Time *(February 20, 1939), "what particularly baffled the pianists, composers and critics who examined the strange invention was this: the keyboard, exactly like that of a piano, yielded not only piano tones but harpsichord tones and simulated effects of many other instruments, such as trumpet, guitar and violin."*

Lillian Petri Horton, who played the Novachord in the orchestra that accompanied the spectacular pageant staged at the Railroads Building, recalls in a 1979 letter to H. A. H. that:

> *Kurt Weill, who wrote the score for the show at Railroads on Parade, was a Novachord enthusiast. He did his*

108

composing on his Novachord and used both Hammond Novachord and Hammond Organ in the orchestra. He hired me and my Novachord to supplement various sections of the orchestra—strings, horns, reeds, or special effects, as needed. The Novachord is an excellent imitator and the forerunner of all the various tonal additions now so common in the most inexpensive of electronic instruments. The Hammond Organ and Hammond Novachord were also used together at the Fair as show piece instruments by Ferde Grofé at the Ford Exhibit.

The Hammond Novachord was essentially the first synthesizer. [It] generates the basic octave frequencies electronically by the use of radio tubes. These frequencies are then further electronically divided to generate the rest of the keyboard notes. Through the use of condensors and resistors controlled by a series of levers located at the front of the instrument, harmonics are then added in various degrees by the musician to produce different types of tones. This is essentially the way the popular synthesizers of today work excepting that transitors have replaced the 144 tubes which are in the Novachord's generator. The Novachord was also one of the first (if not the first) stereo musical instrument, with the sound coming out of each side of the console.

Amusement zone in 1940, showing lighting canopy (cat. no. 119). A new car was given away each day in the Golden Key Contest. (NYP)

A breathless but happy landing on the Parachute Jump. (PMW)

NORMAN BEL GEDDES, designer

122. CRYSTAL GAZING PALACE, 1938.
Pencil on paper, 24 x 19½.
Lent by the Humanities Research Center,
The University of Texas, Austin.

*Bel Geddes, whose background was in theater
design, constructed this concession in the
Amusement zone. Inside, a scantily-clad dancer
performed in a mirrored room where her
image was reflected a thousandfold. Life
reported that red costumes (however
abbreviated) gave the most exciting effect.*

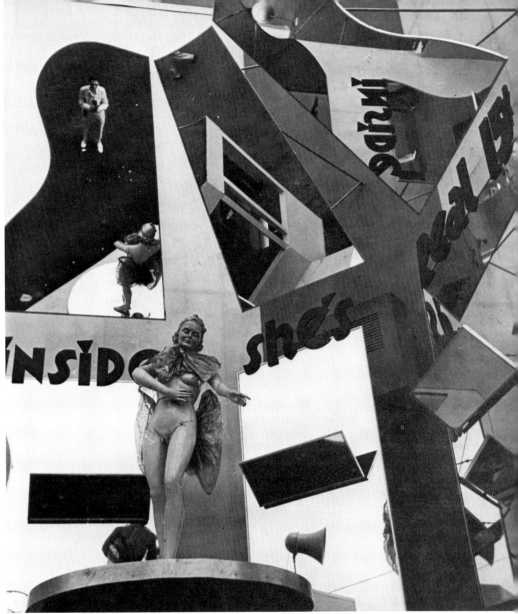

MORGAN, HAMEL AND ENGELKEN, engineers

123. LAGOON OF NATIONS, ELECTRICAL FORMATION OF LIGHTING UNITS AND DISTRIBUTION OF CIRCUIT AND CONTROL WIRES, 1938.
Pencil on tracing paper, 29⅞ x 42.
Dated, lower right: November 26, 1938.
Lent by the Department of Parks, City of New York.

"The New York World's Fair Corporation combines all the decorative, fantastic and spectacular elements — i.e., gas, water, fireworks, light, and sound to present for the first time a synchronized, spectacular show that appeals to all the senses. Consider the magnitude of the undertaking by the realization that the Lagoon of Nations would easily accommodate all of Radio City; that sixty tons of water will be in the air at one time; that more gas is burned in two minutes than Suffolk County burns in an entire evening. Imagine sixty-seven high-powered fire hoses working simultaneously and you will have the effect of one of the rings of this fountain. The geometrical form is that of a three-ringed circus." (Information Manual, February 28, 1939.)

Ticket booth and façade, Crystal Gazing Palace. (BGA)

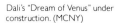
Dali's "Dream of Venus" under construction. (MCNY)

SALVADOR DALI

124. Sketch for Dream of Venus pavilion, 1939.
Tempera and pencil on illustration board,
29⅞ x 40.
Lent by the Ian Woodner Family
Collection.

"In a series of living pictures executed in three dimensions, famed and lively Salvador Dali explains some of the secrets [of Surrealism]. In front of the spectator is a long animated panorama that includes a thirty-foot glass and steel tank filled with water, at the bottom of which is a room from a Dream House. Lovely diving girls plunge into the tank and by their actions seem to reveal the secrets of some dreams. The representation includes Dali's famous 'Soft Watches,' 'Piano Women,' 'Anthropomorphic Seaweed,' 'Exploding Giraffes,' a cow at the bottom of the sea, a couch in the shape of Garbo's lips, and of course his 'Living Liquid Ladies,' Admission 25¢." (Official Guide Book, 1939.)

125. Selection of programs

AMERICAN JUBILEE Souvenir Program,
1940.
Lent by Arthur Cohen.

RAILROADS ON PARADE (music by Kurt
Weill) Souvenir Program, 1939.
The Queens Museum, gift of
Frank Pokorney.

MORRIS GUEST'S MIDGET TOWN
Souvenir Brochure, undated.
The Queens Museum, gift of
Frank Pokorney.

THE STREETS OF PARIS Souvenir
Program, 1939.
Lent by Joseph Cotar.

The American Jubilee. (NYP)

The Aquacade was constructed by the State of New York as a permanent marine amphitheater seating 10,000, with a temporary state exhibit hall at its entrance. The amphitheater was leased to showman Billy Rose, who had premiered his "million dollar" water pageant at the 1936 Great Lakes Exposition in Cleveland. Rose's wife, former Olympic backstroke champion Eleanor Holm, and the equally stellar swimmers Johnny (Tarzan) Weissmuller (1939) and Larry "Buster" Crabbe (1940) headed the cast of some 500 Aquabelles and Aquabeaux plus singers, dancers, and comedy acts. With ticket prices ranging from 40¢ to 99¢, the show grossed more than $4.3 million in its two-season run, making it the most successful of the Amusement zone attractions.

TONY SARG, designer

126. OFFICIAL WORLD'S FAIR PICTORIAL MAP, 1939.
Color offset lithograph, published by Pace Press, Inc.
Lent by Frank Cannavo.

STREETS OF PARIS (featuring Gypsy Rose Lee) Souvenir Program, 1940.
Lent by Alfred N. Reinhardt.

SUN VALLEY/A WINTER WONDERLAND Souvenir Program, 1940.
Lent by Gene Graves.

BILLY ROSE'S AQUACADE (starring Eleanor Holm and Johnny Weissmuller) Souvenir Program, 1939.
The Queens Museum, gift of Frank Pokorney.

YOURS FOR A SONG (Aquacade Theme), sheet music, 1939.
Words by Billy Rose and Ted Fetter, music by Dana Suesse.
Lent by Barry Kogan.

Would-be "Aquabelles" audition for Billy Rose at Madison Square Garden, Spring 1940. (AL)

The Fair's official "Flagmaster" readies flags and banners for opening day. (NYP)

JOSEPH BINDER, designer

127. NEW YORK WORLD'S FAIR 1939/THE WORLD OF TOMORROW.
Color offset lithograph, 30 x 20.
The Queens Museum, gift of Carla Binder.

JOHN ATHERTON, designer

128. NEW YORK WORLD'S FAIR 1939.
Color offset lithograph, 30¼ x 20¼.
Lent by Eugene A. Santomasso.

ALBERT STAEHLE, designer

129. NEW YORK WORLD'S FAIR 1939.
Color offset lithograph, 20 x 13¼.
Lent by Peter M. Warner.

"Destined to be the most widely displayed poster in modern times, the design by Joseph Binder was announced the winner of the New York World's Fair poster competition by Grover A. Whalen, president of the Fair Corporation.

"Two other posters submitted in the competition, one by John Atherton of Ridgefield, Connecticut, the other by Albert Staehle of New York City, were also accepted

The National Cash Register's building registered the daily attendance of the Fair. (NYP)

by the New York World's Fair and will be used in the world-wide promotion campaign.

"...Mr. Binder, who has received many awards and prizes in international competitions for advertising design and who lectures and writes concerning the applied arts, said that only once in a lifetime does an artist get an opportunity to do a poster for as great a subject as the New York World's Fair. He added that it was even rarer for an artist to be provided with a new design form such as the

Trylon and Perisphere.

"'I have been so impressed by the size and magnitude of the Fair that I decided the Trylon and Perisphere should be placed at the top of the world,' Mr. Binder said. 'I felt that New York should appear beside it, but much smaller, and that an indication should be given by the train, ship and planes of the rush of peoples to this greatest of all expositions.'" (Press release, Department of Feature Publicity, November 1938.)

127.

128.

129.

130.

NEMBHARD N. CULIN, designer

130. IN 1939 THE NEW YORK WORLD'S
FAIR, 1937.
Color offset lithograph, 40 x 28.
Lent by the artist.

HOWARD SCOTT, designer

131. MAKES YOU PROUD OF YOUR
COUNTRY/WORLD'S FAIR 1940.
Color offset lithograph, 20 x 13¼.
Lent by Peter M. Warner.

BOB SMITH, designer

132. FOR YOUR SUMMER
VACATION/WORLD'S
FAIR NEW YORK.
Color offset lithograph, 20 x 13¼.
Lent by Peter M. Warner.

S. EKMAR, designer

133. GO BY ALL MEANS/WORLD'S FAIR IN
NEW YORK 1940.
Color offset lithograph, 20 x 13¼.
Lent by Peter M. Warner.

T. P. CHRYSTIE

134. NEW YORK WORLD'S FAIR 1940: Design
for poster.
Tempera on illustration board, 15 x 10.
Lent by Robert Heide and John Gilman.

H. P. BRITE

135. Liberty-head design with Trylon and
Perisphere motif, undated.
Pencil, pastel, and charcoal on illustration
board, 15⅞ x 11¾.
Lent by Robert Heide and John Gilman.

139.

ARTIST UNKNOWN

136. Fifty-four mechanicals for Official Poster
Stamps, published by Nicklin Company,
New York © New York World's Fair
1939, Inc.
Tempera on illustration board with
watercolor and pencil on tracing paper
overlay, each 4 x 6⅛.
Private collection.

137. Official flag, New York World's Fair 1939
Cotton, 58 x 93.
Lent by Frank Cronican.

138. Official flag, New York World's Fair 1940
Cotton, 60 x 96.
The Queens Museum, gift of Frank
Pokorney.

139. WELCOME WORLD'S FAIR VISITORS,
display banner.
Cotton, 36 x 100 (max.).
Lent by Thomas Diddle.

140. WORLD'S FAIR INFORMATION,
advertising banner, Richfield Oil Company.
Color printing on cotton, 35½ x 84.
Lent by Peter M. Warner.

141. Souvenir banner, New York World's Fair
1939
Cotton, 24 x 24.
Lent by Elizabeth Steidel.

142. Pair of vertical banners, New York
World's Fair 1940
Cotton, each 108 x 18.
The Queens Museum, gift of
Clifford Parker.

138.

Utility table and four chairs, enamel and wood, lent by Robert Heide and John Gilman. (RH)

An assortment of patches, buttons, badges and medals. (AL)

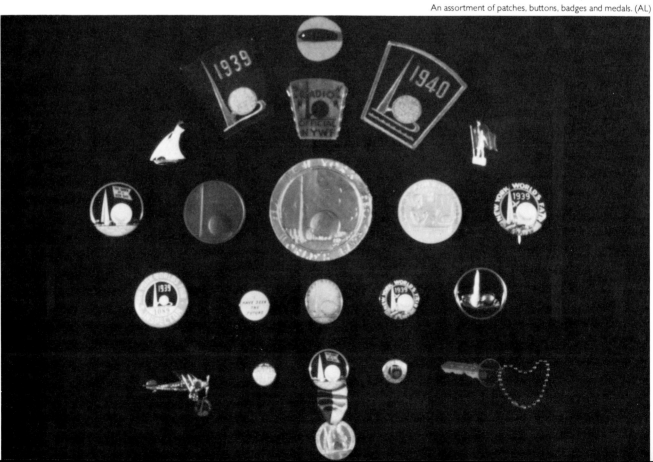

OFFICIAL GUIDE BOOK
NEW YORK WORLD'S FAIR 1939

OFFICIAL GUIDE BOOK

NEW YORK WORLD'S FAIR

OFFICIAL GUIDE BOOK

THE WORLD'S FAIR OF 1940 IN NEW YORK

FOR PEACE AND FREEDOM

Guest of THE NEW YORK WORLD'S FAIR

WORLD'S FAIR OF 1940
The Peace and Freedom
PIERRE TORO
BURNEY

NEW Billy Rose's 1940
Aquacade
ELEANOR HOLM   BUSTER CRABBE

N.Y. WORLD'S FAIR OF 1940
The Peace and Freedom
COTY DAY
JUNE 14

WORLD'S FAIR 1939
SOUVENIR
ELECTRICAL WORKERS
LOCAL UNION NUMBER 3
INTERNATIONAL BROTHERHOOD OF ELECTRICAL WORKERS
AMERICAN FEDERATION OF LABOR
SATURDAY OCTOBER 28, 1939

U. S. CUSTOMS
NEW YORK WORLD'S FAIR
1939
EXHIBIT
ENTRY NO.
WARNING
NOT TO BE OPENED EXCEPT IN THE PRESENCE OF A CUSTOMS OFFICER

A CAR A DAY GIVEN AWAY!
PLYMOUTH, FORD AND CHEVROLET!
WORLD'S FAIR
GOLDEN KEY
CONTEST
SPONSORED BY A GROUP
OF NEW YORK CITY STORES

NEW YORK WORLD'S FAIR 1939
COMBINATION BOOK
OF SOUVENIR TICKETS
PRICE $3.75

WORLD'S FAIR OF 1940
CHASE
BRASS DAY
JUNE 22

The WORLD'S FAIR OF 1940
IN NEW YORK
BOOK OF SOUVENIR TICKETS
$2.50
No. 387500

I AM AN AMERICAN DAY
OCT. 13, 1940
$1.00

Mrs. Harvey Abuhove
American Telephone and Telegraph Company
Kenneth Anger
David Barison
Joseph Beim
Dr. Harry Berenholtz
Carla Binder
Ilya Bolotowsky
Grace Borgenicht Gallery, New York
Anna and Kenneth Brett, Jr.
Stephen Browne
Henry F. Brzezinski
Robert Busch
Frank Cannavo
Reginald Case
Charles Apfelbaum Books, Valley Stream, New York
Dorris Clarke
Arthur Cohen
Consolidated Edison
Cooper-Hewitt Museum, Smithsonian Institution, New York
Joseph Cotar
Mr. G.F. Crabtree
Frank Cronican
Mr. and Mrs. Martin Crowley
Nembhard N. Culin
John D'Amico
Mrs. Stuart Davis
Department of Cultural Affairs, City of New York
Department of Parks, City of New York

Mrs. Gleb Derujinsky
Mr. and Mrs. Martin Diamond
Martin Diamond Fine Arts, Inc., New York
Thomas Diddle
Mrs. Eliot Duhan
Milton M. Duke
E.I. Du Pont de Nemours and Company
Morris Ferrara
Eileen Flynn
Mrs. Seymour Fogel
Sam Fox
The Franklin D. Roosevelt Library, Hyde Park, New York
Ruth Arlene Friend
gallerie a, Sag Harbor, New York
Olive Lyford Gavert
John Gilman
Graham Gallery, New York
Gene Graves
Balcomb Greene
Eleanor Gunderson
Haines, Lundberg and Waehler
Hardesty and Hanover, Consulting Engineers
Mr. W. C. Hausheer
Robert Heide
Robert Gaston Herbert II
Herbert F. Johnson Museum of Art, Cornell University, Ithaca
Joyce Hirschhorn
Hoblitzelle Theatre Arts Library, University of Texas at Austin
Kevin and Brenda Hom
Mr. and Mrs. Charles V. Hooks
Lillian Petri Horton
Philip Humphrey
Kenneth Ippolito
Fanny Karwick
Gertrude Hermann Keinath
Robert A. Kelleher
Sam and Ruth Klein
Barry Kogan
Ethel Krause
James Kurshuk
Barbara E. Leighton
Mr. and Mrs. Edward J. Levine
The Library of Congress, Washington, D.C.
Lillian Lichterman
August Lind
Mr. and Mrs. Charles Locasto
Michael Loew
Connie Lohse
Thomas G. Lo Medico
Harry I. Losin
Carol McCulley
Marlborough Fine Art (London) Ltd.

Josephine Melendez
Museum of the City of New York
Nassau County Office of Cultural Development
Benjamin Nathan
National Collection of Fine Arts, Smithsonian Institution
The New York Post
The New York Public Library, Astor, Lenox and Tilden Foundations
Joseph Nicotra
David Oats
Stefani O'Connor
Allen L. Palanker
Clifford T. Parker
Marion L. Parker
Nathaniel Platt and Muriel Drummond Platt
Frank Pokorney
Thelma Ulricksen Polito
Portledge School, Locust Valley, New York
Public Buildings Service, General Services Administration
M. Morgan Rawlins
Mirjam Ketonen Rawson
Alfred N. Reinhardt
Research Center for the Federal Theatre Project, George Mason University
Mrs. Michael Rogovin
Clifford Ross
Michael Ross
Peter Rothholz
Mr. and Mrs. Michael Rubinstein
Ralph Russo
Beverly and Ray Sacks
Salander-O'Reilly Galleries, New York
Eugene A. Santomasso
Harold Serva
Audrey T. Shaloo
Philip Shapiro
Mildred and Robert Silverstein
Jerry Simelson
Alex Siodmak
Spaced Gallery, New York
Sandra Sperber
Herbert Starkman
Elizabeth Steidel
Dr. James R. Sweeney
Walter Dorwin Teague Associates, Inc.
Mr. and Mrs. Stuyvesant Van Veen
Peter M. Warner
May Weitze
Westinghouse Electric Corporation
Doris Wight
John C. Witek
Helen Wittenberg
Ian Woodner Family Collection

Barbara Collishaw in the Kodak Garden of Photography, June 5, 1939. (MR)

Alex Siodmak

Dan Brinzak, Grace Borgenicht Gallery: 29
Courtesy of Stephen Browne: (SB)
Courtesy of Henry Brzezinski: (HB)
Courtesy of Frank Cronican: (FC)
Nembhard Culin: (NC)
Roselle Davis: (RD)
Martin Diamond Fine Arts: 50
T. Lux Feininger: (TLF)
Franklin D. Roosevelt Library: 24
Graham Galleries: 101
Balcomb Greene: 54
Courtesy of Helen A. Harrison: (HAH)
Robert Heide: (RH)
Gertrude Keinath: (GK)
Alan Law: 7, 9, 15-18, 23, 24, 28, 31, 35, 36, 38, 61, 62, 82, 95, 99, 100, 103, (AL)

Library of Congress, Samuel Gottscho Collection: (LC)
Michael Loew: (ML)
Harry Losin: (HL)
Marlborough Fine Arts (London) Ltd.: 34, 96-98
Museum of the City of New York: (MCNY)
National Archives: (NA)
National Collection of Fine Arts: 11, 44
Courtesy of the National Sculpture Society: (NSS)
The New York *Post*: (NYP)
New York Public Library Picture Collection: (NYPL)
Norman Bel Geddes Archive, University of Texas: (BGA)

Courtesy of Francis V. O'Connor: (FVO'C)
Public Buildings, General Services Administration: 108, 109
Radio Corporation of America: (RCA)
Courtesy of Michael Ross: (MR)
Sacks Fine Arts: 8
Salander-O'Reilly Galleries: 42
Eugene A. Santomasso: (EAS)
Alex Siodmak: (AS)
Walter Dorwin Teague Associates: (WDT)
Courtesy of Stuyvesant Van Veen: (SVV)
Courtesy of Peter M. Warner: (PMW)
Westinghouse Corporation: 1
Works Progress Administration: WPA

A Fair guide instructs American Airlines stewardesses in describing the exposition from the air. (NYP)

Demolition of the American Tobacco Company's
"Lucky Strike" Building, winter, 1940. (NYP)